MW00983663

Let's Talk
Arabic

Adam Yacoub

http://www.LetsTalkArabic.com/
This title is also available at the major online book retailers.
© Copyright 2011 Dr. Adam Yacoub
ISBN-13: 978-1467968744
ISBN-10: 1467968749

DEDICATION

I wish to thank all of those who have kindly helped with developing this book. Every effort or advice have been made to trace all the covered topics but if any have been inadvertently overlooked the author will be pleased to make the necessary arrangements at first opportunity.

Contents

Visit the link to look inside http://www.LetsTalkArabic.com

www.LetsTalkArabic.com

ACKNOWLEDGMENTS

I'm lucky enough to have benefited from the experience of some of the experts in teaching Arabic across this edition. I would like to thank everyone for their useful comments on this work

Part 1

VISIT THIS LINK TO LOOK INSIDE THE BOOK

www.LetsTalkArabic.com

Preface
Congratulations

mabrook

Well done for making the decision to learn the Arabic language. Whatever your reason – a new challenge, relocation to an Arabic speaking country or for business – you can rest assured that you have made a great decision by choosing one of the most successful and smoothest Arabic courses. This book will lead you to push yourself enabling you to take a step above the rest in a fun and interactive way.

Arabic is considered one of the most animated, important and beautiful languages in the world. This book uses an extremely stimulating, logical and easy way to help you learn from the very beginning. In learning any language, speaking appears to be the most fundamental aspect for most of people. From the beginning of this book, you will be introduced to the basics of speaking and pronunciation using a simple format that allows everyone to speak Arabic in a natural way. The book will then continue to develop your new skills by enabling you to understand and heighten your ability to read, listen to and write this amazing language.

Arabic is a Semitic language; it is the formal and official language of 22 Arab countries, and the spoken language of almost 420 million people living in Arabic and non-Arabic countries.

This book will teach you the basics of Modern Standard Arabic (MSA), which is the modernization of the Classical Arabic structures, it will also teach you some additional phrases from the main dialects spoken all over the Arab world.

Variations of the Language

Like any other language, spoken Arabic has dialects with variations and differences. The differences between these dialects make it incomprehensible to speakers of another dialect. The five main dialects are divided according to their regions.

Maghreb: The Maghreb dialect is spoken in the region of the Maghreb countries: Libya, Tunisia, Algeria, Mauritania, and Morocco.

Egyptian: The Egyptian dialect is used in Egypt, Sudan, Yemen, and some western parts of Saudi Arabia. It is the most widely understood colloquial dialect across the Arab world because approximately 93% of Arabic movies, TV, and media use the Egyptian dialect.

Levantine: The Levantine dialect comes from and is used in Lebanon, Palestine, Jordan and Syria.

The Gulf: The Gulf dialect is spoken in the Arab Gulf countries, which are made up of Iraq, Kuwait, most of Saudi Arabia, Qatar, Bahrain, the United Arab Emirates, and Oman.

Modern Standard Arabic: MSA (Modern Standard Arabic) has become the most popular dialect and is now used by all Arab countries.

The dark colored countries on the map show the Arab League.

Written Arabic: The core of Arabic writing that is used today comes from the classical Arabic, which is the Arabic used in the Qur'an and in the earliest form of literature from the Arabian Peninsula.

Two Important Facts

The first point is that although every language has a vast wealth of vocabulary, we don't need to learn all the vocabulary to be able to communicate in any given language.

<u>Just 20%</u> of the words in a language make up to <u>80%</u> of the conversations we face in our daily life. After learning 20% of the language, you may not be able to speak like a native immediately, but you'll have a solid base and the ability to keep improving and developing yourself. This method is suitable for everyone from frequent travellers to first timers, language students and enthusiasts.

This book focuses on the vital 20% that will help you to speak Arabic interactively and dynamically.

The second – really exciting – point is that the Arabic language uses word roots. For example, we can take one root like **KTB** from the word **KaTaBa**, which means "he wrote", and from there conjugate all **Arabic verbs tense.** Nouns can also be made from the same root because they have a relation with it.

KaaTeB = writer,   **KeTaab** = book,   ma**KTaB** = office,

ma**KTaBa** = library,   ma **KToob** = letter & written,   and more.

Arabic grammar is fairly simple compared to Western languages, but the language itself has richness in its vocabulary that exceeds most languages in the Western world.

The Transliteration

Below is the Arabic alphabet and the key to show you how to pronounce the letters in words. Try to pay attention to the pronunciation as you read.

Pronunciation	The letter
As in (a); apple, absolutely, April, and like (a): man, hat, mat.	ا Alif ('a)
As in (b); bat, band, balcony.	ب Ba' (b)
As in (t); tank, tab.	ت Ta' (t)
Like (th); thank, three, throat, thin, think, thief.	ث Tha' (th)
As in (j): Jam, jack, jacket.	ج Jeem (j)
A rough, aspirated ' H ' (as when you swallowed something hot), or when you breath after running or doing sports Not in English	ح (H)
As in (loch) in Scottish English accent,	خ Kha' (kh)

As in (d); dad, door, dean.	د Dal (d)
Like (th): they, father, mother, brother, together, feather.	ذ Thal (Th)
As in (r): run, role, real.	ر Ra' (r)
As in (z): zoo, zone.	ز Zai (z)
As in (s): sat, sink, soon.	س Seen (s)
Like (sh): shark, she, shy, Sharon.	ش Sheen (sh)
Heavy consonant of (s) like: son, summer.	ص Saad (S)
Heavy consonant of (d) like in: done, duck	ض Daad (D)
Heavy consonant of (T) like: Tariq, tall, tower	ط Taa' (T)
Heavy consonant of the letter (z), sounds similar to although	ظ (TH) Not in English
Not in English, it's roughly like (ai) in main but stronger	ع (A) Ain
Like the French (r)	غ (gh)ghain
As in (f): farm, film, fogy, family	ف (f) Fa'
Like (q): Qatar, Qur'an, quality.	ق (q) qaf
Like (k): kind, king, Kuwait.	ك (k) Kaf
As in (l): lamp, lane, language.	ل (l) lam
As in (m): man, milk, moon.	م (m) Meem
As in (n): now, new, nominal.	ن (n) Noon
Like (h): hand, hair, here, honey, hear.	ه (h) Ha'
Like (o): one, and (o) in: moon, more.	و (w) waw
Like (y): you, yesterday, and like (i) in: him, drink, Friday.	ي (y) Yaa'

UNIT ONE

Saying "Hello"

UNIT ONE

Saying "Hello"

Contents

- Dialogue: *Saying "Hello"*

- Vocabulary

- Other useful phrases

- Culture notes: *Greetings in Arabic*

- Vocabulary practice

- Grammar and usage: The *verb "to be" in Arabic*
                        Definite and indefinite articles
                        Gender

- Exercises

Hello!

as-salaamu Aalaykum!

السَّلامُ عَلَيْكُم!

In this lesson you will learn some basic greetings and how to ask "How are you?"

Dialogue: Adam meets an old high school friend, Mahmoud. They haven't seen each other for a long time.

English	Transliteration	Arabic
Adam: Welcome Mahmoud!	*A; as-salaamu Aalaykum, marHaban mahmoud!*	آدَم: السَّلامُ عَلَيْكُم؛ مَرْحَباً مَحْمود!
Mahmoud: Hello Adam!	*M: wa Aalaykum as-salaam, 'ahlan wa sahlan ya 'adam!*	مَحْمود: وَعَلَيْكُم السَّلام؛ أَهْلاً وَسَهْلاً يا آدَم!
Adam: How are you?	*A: kayf al-Haal?*	آدَم: كَيْفَ الْحَال؟
Mahmoud: I'm doing well. And you? How are you?	*M: al-Hamdulillah? wa 'anta, kayf al-Haal?*	مَحْمود: الحَمْدُ لله. وَأَنْتَ؟ كَيْفَ الْحَال ؟
Adam: Fine. I'm doing well. Thanks.	*A: al-Hamdu lillah. 'anaa bekhayr. shukran*	آدَم:الحَمْدُ لله. أَنَا بِخَير. شُكْراً.

Vocabulary

English	Transliteration	Arabic
peace	*as-salaam*	السَّلام
peace be upon you!	*as-salaamu Aalaykum*	السَّلام عَلَيْكُم!
and	*wa*	وَ
and upon you peace	*wa Aalaykum as-salaam*	وَعَلَيْكُم السَّلام
how?	*kayf?*	كَيْف؟

how are you?	Kayfa alHaal?	كَيْفَ الْحَال ؟
condition	al-Haal	الْحَال
I / I'm	'anaa	أنا
you (for male)	'anta	أنْتَ
you (for female)	'anti	أنْتِ
praise	al-Hamd	الحَمْد
thanks to God	al-Hmdu lillah	الحَمْدُ لِله
good	khayr	خَيْر
I'm fine	'anaa bekhayr	أنا بِخَيْر
welcome	marHaban	مَرْحَباً
hi	'ahlan	أهْلاً
hello	'ahlan wa-sahlan	أهْلاً وَسَهْلاً
O; Adam	yaa adam	يا آدَم

Continue to other useful phrases

English	Transliteration	Arabic
morning	SabaaH	صَباحْ
good morning	SabaaH el-khayr	صَباح الخَيْر
evening	masaa'	مَساء
good evening	masaa' el-khayr	مَساء الخَيْر
response for good morning	SabaaH en-nuur	صَباح النّور

response for good evening	masaa' en-nuur	مَساء الْنّور
light	en-nuur	الْنّور
daytime	en-nahaar	الْنّهار
night	al-layl	الْلَيل
a night	layla	لَيْلة
nights	layaal	ليال
a day	yawm	يَوْم
days	'ay-yaam	أيّام
today	al-yawm	الْيَوْم
yes	naAam	نَعم
no	laa	لا
The (Definite article).	al	الـ
go with peace	maAa as-salaama	مَعَ السَّلامَة
good night	layla saAiida	لَيْلة سَعيدة
happy	saAiid/saAiida	سَعيد/ سَعيدة
wake up in good condition	tuSbeH Aalaa khayr	تُصْبِح عَلَى خَيْر

Culture Notes

The most common greeting in Arabic is the phrase "*as-salaamu Aalaykum*", which means literally, "May peace be upon you". The most common reply is "*wa Aalaykum as-salaam*", which means literally, "And upon you peace".

But, as you can see in the above phrases, to learn a language you must also learn its culture, because the literal or direct translation may not immediately make sense.

For example, the usual response to the phrase "*SabaaH el-khayr*" (good morning) is "*Sabaah en-nuur.*" "*nuur*" translates literally into "light". This is how Arabs greet each other, because if you greet me using good words, I must greet you using better words!

Also, there is no specific word for greeting someone in the afternoon. You can use either "*as-salaamu Aalaykum*" at any time, or "*masaa' el-khayr*" for the afternoon as well.

Grammar usage

1- The Verb "to be" in Arabic:

In Arabic, there is no direct translation of "**to be**" in the present tense. That means that "**am, is and are**" don't exist in Arabic sentence. For example,

How "**are**" you?	*Kayf al-Haal?*	كَيْفَ الْحَال؟
"**I'm**" doing well. And you? How "are" you?	*al-Hamdu lillah. Wa 'anta, kayf al-Haal?*	الحَمْدُ لِله. وَأنْتَ؟ كَيْفَ الْحَال ؟
Fine. "**I'm**" doing well. Thanks.	*al-Hamdu lillah. 'anaa bekhayr. shukran*	الحَمْدُ لِله. أَنَا بِخَيْر. شُكْراً.

2-Definite and Indefinite articles:

There are no indefinite articles ("a" or "an") in Arabic. For example, "*SabaaH*" means "morning" and "a morning", and "*masaa'*" means "evening" and "an evening".

Arabic has a definite article (like "the" in English). In Arabic, it is "*al*", which is added to the beginning of a word as a prefix. For example, "*al-masaa'*" means "the evening", "*al-Haal*" means "the condition" of someone's health.

There is one other important rule to keep in mind when it comes to the definite article "*al*".

Remember the phrases "*as-salaam*" and "*an-nuur*"? Both "*as*" (in "*as-salaam*") and "*an*" (in "*an-nuur*") mean "the" as well, but neither are pronounced as "*al*". That's because we have found few letters (14 of the 28) in Arabic when they come after the definite article "*al*", so they can cancel the pronunciation of the "*l*" sound in "*al*", in this case you will find only the "*a*" followed by those mentioned letters doubled. Hence, "*as-salaam*" with a double "*s*", and "*an-nuur*" with a double "*n*".

These letters are called "sun letters", because the word "*shams*" in Arabic, which means "sun" also begins with one of them.

How to identify these letters? Simply, they are the ones that we need to use the tip of the tongue to pronounce: *t , th , d , dh , r , z , sh , s, l, n.* :

ت، ث، د، ذ، ر، ز، س، ش، ص، ض، ط، ظ، ل، ن

The other 14 letters that don't force "*l*" in "*al*" to be silent are called "moon letters", because the word "moon" in Arabic (*qamar*) begins with one of them. Here is the example for both cases:

SabaaH = a morning, *aS-SabaaH* = the morning, *masaa'* = an evening, *al-masaa'* = the evening, *shams* = sun, *ash-shams* = the sun, *qamar* = moon, *al-qamar* = the moon.

(You will find further explanation later on in the reading course in Part 2 of this book).

3-Gender:

Arabic is a language that has genders, as does Spanish, French, and Italian. That means every noun is either masculine or feminine.

Nouns that end with the sound "a" – called in Arabic *taa' marbuuta* – are 90% feminine (f). If they end in anything else, they are generally masculine (m). Examples are as follows:

rajul: رَجُل man (m), *walad:* وَلَد boy (m), *mar'a:* مَرْأة woman (f), *ketaab:* كِتاب book (m), *Taawila:* طاولة table (f), *qalam:* قَلَم pen (m), *say-yaara:* سَيّارة car (f). Bear in mind that not all feminine nouns end with this "a" sound.

Examples:

bent: بِنْت girl (f), *ukht:* أُخْت sister (f), *shams:* شَمْس sun (f), *'arD:* أرض earth (f). Note that this type of feminine gender is very rare in Arabic.

It is always better to do an exercise for anything you learn. So if you feel that you are not yet ready to do it, so it is better to get back and read the grammar notes again.

Exercise 1: Match each word in (**A**) with an appropriate word in (**B**) to make a phrase or sentence, go from right to left. **Remember to say the words out loud.**

B		**A**	
bekhayr	بِخَيْر	Aalaykum	عَلَيْكُم
an-nuur	النّور	SabaaH	صَباح
al-khayr	الخَيْر	'anaa	أنا
Aalaykum	عَلَيْكُم	al-Hamdu	الحَمْدُ
assalaamu	السَلامُ	SabaaH	صَباح
al-Haal	الْحَال	Kayf?	كَيف؟
Aala khayr	عَلَى خَيْر	as-salaamu	السَّلامُ
as-salaama	السَّلامَة	layla	لَيْلة
saAiida	سَعيدة	maAa	مَعَ
lillah	لِله	tusbeH	تُصْبِح

22

Exercise 2: What does it mean?

....	marHaban	مَرْحَباً
....	'ahlan	أَهْلاً
....	'ahlan wa-sahlan	أَهْلاً وَسَهْلاً
....	SabaaH el-khayr	صَباح الخَيْر
....	masaa' el-khayr	مَساء الخَيْر
....	maAa as-salaama	مَعَ السَّلامَة
....	tuSbeH Aalaa khayr	تُصْبِح عَلَى خَيْر
....	kayfa alHaal	كَيْفَ الْحَال ؟
....	al-Hmdu lillah	الحَمْدُ لله
....	as-salaamu Aalaykum	السَّلام عَلَيْكُم!
....	wa Aalaykum as-salaam	وَعَلَيْكُم السَّلام

Exercise 3: Fill in the blanks using the vocabulary you have learned, to make a dialogue.

English	Transliteration	Arabic
A: Welcome!	**A**;	.... :آ
B: Hello!	**B**: wa Aalaykum as-salaam, 'ahlan wa sahlan!	ب: وَعَلَيْكُم السَّلام؛ أَهْلاً وَسَهْلاً!
A: How are you?	**A**.....................?	آ: .... ؟
B: I'm doing well. And you. How are you?	**B**: al-Hamdulillah. Wa 'anta, kayf al-Haal?	ب: الحَمْدُ لله. وَأَنْتَ: كَيْفَ الْحَال ؟
A: Fine. I'm doing well. Thanks.	**A**.....................	آ: ....

Exercise 4: **Change these indefinite nouns into definite ones**, using the appropriate form of the article (*al*). Then translate them into English: Remember the rule of the sun letters.

خَيْر	لَيْلة	مَساء	صَباح	يَوْم
khayr	layla	masaa'	SabaaH	yawm
....	....	....	....	....

مَرأة	بِنْت	رَجُل	نَهار	حَال
mar'a	bent	rajul	nahaar	Haal
....	....	....	....	....

Exercise 5: Circle the feminine nouns in the words below.

سَيّارة	لَيْلة	قَلَم	كِتاب	يَوْم
say-yara	layla	qalam	kitaab	yawm

مَرأة	بِنْت	رَجُل	نَهار	أخْت
mar'a	bent	rajul	nahaar	ukht

Exercise 6: Choose the correct Arabic meanings for the English words/phrases below.

A- Hello

3- أَهْلاً 'ahlan	2- مَعَ السَّلامَة maAa as-salaama	1- مَساء الخَيْر masaa' el-khayr

b- Good morning

3- مَساء الخَيْر masaa' el-khayr	2- صَباح الخَيْر SabaaH el-khayr	1- مَعَ السَّلامَة maAa as-salaama

c- Good-bye

3- صَباح الخَيْر SabaaH el-khayr	2- مَعَ السَّلامَة maAa as-salaama	1- أَهْلاً 'ahlan

d- Good evening

3- أَهْلاً 'ahlan	2- مَعَ السَّلامَة maAa as-salaama	1- مَساء الخَيْر masaa' el-khayr

e- Good night

3- مَعَ السَّلامَة maAa as-salaama	2- تُصْبِح عَلَى خَيْر tuSbeH Aalaa khayr	1- أَهْلاً وَسَهْلاً 'ahlan wa-sahlan

f- Welcome

3- صَباح الخَيْر SabaaH el-khayr	2- مَرْحَباً marHaban	1- تُصْبِح عَلَى خَيْر tuSbeH Aalaa khayr

Exercise 7: Translate into Arabic.

1- Hello, good morning

....

2- Hi, good evening

....

3- Good afternoon

....

4- The response for good morning

....

5- The response for good evening

....

6- Welcome

....

7- How are you?

....

8- I'm fine, Thanks.

....

9- Good night

....

10- Good-bye

....

Exercise 8: Put the words in the correct order to make a phrase or sentence. Don't forget to go from right to left.

السَّلامُ	مَرْحَباً	عَلَيْكُم	يا آدَم	-1
as-salaamu	marHaban	Aalaykum	ya 'adam	
....	....	....	....	
السَّلام	وَعَلَيْكُم	وَسَـهْلاً	أهْلاً	-2
as-salaam	wa Aalaykum	wa sahlan	'ahlan	
....	....	....	....	
الْحَال	كَيْفَ	؟		-3
al-Haal	Kayf			
....	....			
لِله	الحَمْدُ	شُكْراً	بِخَير	-4
lillah	al-Hamdu	shukran	bekhayr	
....	....	....	....	

Exercise 9: Complete your first Arabic crossword puzzle! Write down the Arabic meaning for the words below.

Down

1- Day

2- The Condition

Cross

3- Evening   5- Peace

4- Morning

Exercise 10: Can you find four words you have learned in the word square as in the example? Go from right to left.

1- *Morning*.......................

2- *Evening*.......................

3- *Welcome*...................

4- *Hello*....................................

5- *Peace*.........................

ظ	غ	ع	ح	ا	ب	ص
ء	ا	س	م	ت	ي	ب
ا	ب	ح	ر	م	ا	ى
ة	س	ر	ا	ل	ه	ا
م	ا	ل	س	ص	ج	د

Vocabulary

السَّلام
as-salaam,peace

السَّلام عَلَيْكُم
as-salaamu Aalaykum,peace be upon you!

وَ
wa,and

وَعَلَيْكُم السَّلام
wa Aalaykum as-salaam,and upon you peace

كَيْفَ؟
kayf?,how?

كَيْفَ الْحَال؟
Kayfa alHaal?,how are you?

الْحَال
al-Haal,condition

أنا
'anaa,I / I'm

أَنْتَ
'anta,you (for male)

أُنْتِ
'anti,you (for female)

الحَمْد
al-Hamd,praise

الحَمْدُ للہ
al-Hmdu lillah,thanks to God

خَيْر
khayr,good

الـ
al,The (Definite article).

مَعَ السَّلامَة
maAa as-salaama,goodbye

أَيْلَة سَعِيدة
layla saAiida,good night

سَعِيد / سَعِيدة
saAiid/saAiida,happy

تُصْبِح عَلَى خَيْر
tuSbeH Aalaa khayr,wake up in good condition

رَجُل
rajul,man

وَلَد
walad,boy

بِنْت
bent,girl

كِتَاب
ketaab,book

قَلَم
qalam,pen

سَيَّارة
say-yaara,car

طَاوِلة
Taawela,table

أرض

أنا بِخَير
'anaa bekhayr,I'm fine
مَرْحَباً
marHaba,welcome
أَهْلاً
'ahlan,hi
أَهْلاً وَسَهْلاً
'ahlan wa-sahlan,hello
نَعَم
naAam,yes
لا
laa,no
صَباح
SabaaH,morning
صَباح الخَير
SabaaH el-khayr,good morning
مَساء
masaa',evening
مَساء الخَير
masaa' el-khayr,good evening
صَباح النَّور
SabaaH en-nuur,response for good morning
مَساء النَّور
masaa' en-nuur,response for good evening
النَّور
en-nuur,light
النَّهار
en-nahaar,daytime

'arD,earth
أُخت
ukht,sister
اللَّيل
al-layl,night
لَيْلة
layla,a night
يَوْم
yawm,a day
لَيال
layaale,nights
أَيَّام
'ay-yaam,days
اليَوْم
al-yawm,today

UNIT TWO
What's your name?

UNIT TWO

What's your name?

Contents

- Dialogue Two: *"What's your name?"*

- Vocabulary

- Other useful vocabulary

- Things around us

- Grammar notes

- The possessive adjective
  Subject pronouns
  Question words

- Exercises

What is your name?

maa esmuk?

ما اِسْمُك؟

Dialogue: Adam meets John for first time at the university. They get to know each other.

English	Transliteration	Arabic
Adam: Welcome!	*A: marHaban.*	آدَم: مَرْحَباً.
John: Hello!	*B: 'ahlan wa sahlan.*	جون: أهْلاً وَسَهْلاً.
Adam: My name is Adam, What is your name, please?	*A: esmii 'adam. maa esmuka men faDlek?*	آدَم: اِسْمي آدَم، ما اِسْمُك مِنْ فَضْلِك؟
John: My name is John!	*B: esmii john.*	جون: اِسْمي جون.
Adam: Are you from France?	*A: 'anta men faransaa?.*	آدم: أنْتَ مِنْ فَرَنْسا؟
John: No. I'm American from Boston. Where are you from?	*B: laa. 'anaa 'amriikyy men madiinat boston, wa men ayn 'anta?*	جون:لا، أنا أمْريكي مِنْ مَدينة بوسطن، وَمِنْ أيْن أنْتَ؟
Adam: I'm Egyptian from Cairo.	*A: 'anaa meSryy men madiinat el-qaahera.*	آدَم: أنا مِصْري مِنْ مِدينَة القاهِرَة.
John: Nice to meet you, Adam.	*B: furSa saAiida yaa 'adam!*	جون: فُرْصَة سَعيدَة يا آدم.
Adam: Nice to meet you.	*A: tashar-rafna*	آدَم: تَشَرَّفْنا.

Vocabulary followed by unhighlighted sentences as an example

English	Transliteration	Arabic
name	esm	اِسْم
my name	esmii	اِسْمي
esmii Adam		اِسْمي آدم
what's your name?	maa esmuk?	ما اِسْمُك؟
please	men faDlek	مِنْ فَضْلِك
maa esmuk men faDlek?		ما اسمك من فضلك؟
if you would	law samaHt	لَوْ سَمَحْت
maa esmuk law samHt?		ما اسمك لو سَمَحت؟
country	balad	بَلَد
baladii meSr		بَلَدي مِصر
Arab	Aarabyy	عَرَبي
'anta Aarabyy?		أنتَ عَربي؟
from	men	مِنْ
where	'ayn	أيْن
in	fii	في
American	'amriikyy	أَمْريكِيّ
Egyptian	meSryy	مِصْرِيّ
men 'ayn 'anta?		مِن أين أنتَ؟

'ayn adam?		أين آدم؟
adam fii meSr		آدم في مِصر
Nice to meet you	*furSa saAiida*	قُرْصَة سَعِيدَة
Honored to meet you	*tashar-rafna*	تَشَرّفْنا
tashar-rafna ya sara		تشرفنا يا سارة.

Things around us

English	Transliteration	Arabic
chair	*kursii*	كُرسي
men 'ayn alkursii?		مِن أين الكُرسي؟
men as-suuq.		مِن السوق.
book	*ketaab*	كِتاب
men 'ayn haTha alketaab?		مِن أين هذا الكتاب؟
office/ desk	*maktab*	مَكْتَب
'ayn 'anta? 'anaa fii elmaktab		أين أنت؟ أنا في المكتب
table	*Taawela*	طَاوِلة
on	*Aalaa*	عَلَى
computer	*Haaseb*	حاسِب
'ayn al-Haaseb? Aalaa aT-Taawela		أين الحاسب؟ على الطاولة
seat	*meqAad*	مِقْعَد
room	*ghurfa*	غُرْفَة
'ayn almeqAad? fii el-ghurfa.		أين المقعد؟ في الغُرفة.
home	*bayt*	بَيْت
'ayna 'anta? 'anaa fii el-bayt		أين أنتَ؟ أنا في البيت
classroom	*faSl*	فَصْل
sara fii el-faSl		سارة في الفصل
school	*madrasa*	مَدْرَسَة
'ayna alketaab? fii el-madrasa		أين الكتاب؟ في المدرسة

university	*jaameAa*	جَامِعَة
Ahmad fii el-jaameAa		أحمد في الجامعة
college/ faculty	*kul-ley-ya*	كُلّية
'anaa fii el-kul-ley-ya		أنا في الكُلّية
city/ town	*madiina*	مَدِينة
'ayn madiina doha?		أين مدينة الدوحة؟
street	*shaare'*	شارِع
al-bayt fii haTha ash-shaare'		البيت في هذا الشارع
message	*resaala*	رِسَالة
ar-resaala Aalaa al-maktab		الرسالة على المكتب
address	*unwaan*	عُنوان
haThaa al-unwaan? nAam		هذا العنوان؟ نَعَم
area/ region	*menTaqa*	مِنطقة
people	*an-naas*	الناس
an-naas fii haThehe el-menTaqa Aarab		الناس في هذه المنطقة عرب

Grammar notes

By now you should be able to recognize many words from the previous lesson. Remember the very common greeting phrase in Arabic "*marHaban*" and "*'ahlan wa sahlan*"; these are the friendly phrases that Mahmoud and Adam used.

To ask someone, "What's your name?" simply say: "*maa esmuka?*" to a man, or "*maa esmuke?*" to a woman. Word by word: "maa" means: (what) and (your) is a possessive pronoun, which consists of (you = *'anta* or *'ante*) with the addition of "*ka* or *ke*" to give the meaning of "*esmuka*" for a man or "*esmuke*" for a woman. Remember that Arabic doesn't express is, are, or am, and there are two forms of you: "*anta*" to a man, and "*anti*" to a woman. The response for this question is "My (possessive pronoun) + name", which, in Arabic, becomes "*esm + ii*".

How do you ask: "Where are you from?" simply say "*men 'ayn 'anta?*" to a man, as we mentioned above, or use "*'ante*" to a woman. There are different forms for speaking to two people, or three or more, but do not worry about that for now!

After practicing this dialogue, you will have learned how to speak in a friendly to anyone and be able to use a useful phrase like "*furSa saAiida*" or "*tashar-rafna*", which means "nice to meet you".

1- The possessive adjective

Where are you from?

The title refers to a type of adjective formed by adding a suffix "*yy*" for masculine or "*y-ya*" for feminine nouns. **To form the nationality for a place or noun, follow these steps:**

1- Remove the definite article if the noun has an *al*, as in the examples.

2- Remove *alif* or *taa' marbuuta* from the end of the noun if it has either.

3- Add the suffix *yy* to make the adjective for male, or *y-ya* to make it for female. See the following:

English	Female adjective (nationality)	Male adjective (nationality)	Country	
Egyptian	مِصْرِيّة *meSrey-ya*	مِصْرِيّ *meSryy*	مِصْر *meSr*	
Syrian	سُوريّة *Suury-ya*	سُوريّ *suuryy*	سُورية *suurya*	
Lebanese	لُبْنانيّة *lubnaaney-ya*	لُبْنانيّ *lubnaanyy*	لُبْنان *lubnaan*	
Canadian	كَنَديّة *kanadey-ya*	كَنَدي *kanadyy*	كَنَدا *kanada*	
Iraqi	عِراقيّة *Aeraaqey-ya*	عِراقيّ *Aeraaqyy*	العِراق *al-Aeraaq*	
French	فَرَنْسِيّة *faransey-ya*	فَرَنْسيّ *faransyy*	فَرِنْسا *faransaa*	
German	ألمانيّة *'almaaney-ya*	ألمانيّ *'almaanyy*	ألمانيا *'almaanya*	

2-Subject pronouns

Arabic is like English; it has two sets of personal pronouns: subject and possessive pronouns. There is some overlap among these sets. However, Arabic has more pronouns than English (formal Arabic has separate categories for masculine and feminine and dual pronouns for sets of two, these are not used in most varieties of spoken Arabic). Here you will learn the most commonly used subject pronouns in spoken Arabic:

I	'anaa	أنا	First person
We	naHnu	نَحْنُ	
You (for male)	'anta	أنْتَ	Second person
You (for female)	'anti	أنْتِ	
You (plural)	'antum	أنتُم	
He / It (for masculine)	huwa	هُوَ	Third person
She /It (for feminine)	heya	هِيَ	
They (plural)	hum	هُم	

Examples

'anaa hunaa	أنا هُنا
naHnu fii el-bayt	نَحْنُ في البيت
'anta meSryy?	أنْتَ مِصْري؟
'anti 'amriikyya?	أنْتِ أمريكية؟
'antum men Oman? naAam	أنتُم مِن عُمان؟ نَعم
huwa men al-yaman	هُوَ مِن اليمن
heya men Qatar	هِيَ مِن قَطَر
hum men lybya	هُم مِن ليبيا

Say it in Arabic

1- I'm at home

2- We are in the market

3- Are you (Male) here?

4- Are you (Female) there?

5- Are you (all) from Egypt?

6- he is in the office

7- she is at home

8- they are here

Fill in the blanks with the appropriate pronouns

1- esmii John .... ana men madiinat NewYork
1- اِسمي جون؛ .... من مدينة نيويورك

2- men 'ayn .... ya Sara?
2- مِن أيْن .... يا سارة؟

3- 'ayna Adam? .... fii el-bayt
3- أين آدم؟ .... في البيت

4- men 'ayn Nicol? .... men faransa
4- مِنْ أين نيكول؟ .... مِن فَرَنسا

5- men 'ayn .... yaa Adam?
5- مِن أين .... يا آدم؟

6- men 'ayn ....? hum men Qatar
6- مِن أين ....؟ هُم مِن قَطَر

7- men 'ayn 'antum? .... men al-yaman
7- مِن أين أنتم؟ .... مِن اليَمَن

3- Question words

To ask a question in Arabic, use one of the words below at the beginning of a sentence:

English	Transliteration	Arabic
What? (used before nouns)	maa	ما؟
What? (used before verbs)	maaThaa	ماذا؟
Why?	lema / lemaaThaa	لِمَ / لِماذا؟
Where?	'ayn	أيْن؟
Who?	man	مَنْ؟
When?	mataa	مَتى؟
How?	kayf	كَيْف؟
For (Yes/No) question	hal	هل؟
From where?	men 'ayn	مِنْ أين؟
Which?	'ayy	أي؟

Examples:

English	Transliteration	Arabic
What is this?	maa haThaa?	ما هذا؟
What do you do?	maaThaa taAmal?	ماذا تَعمَل؟
Why are you at home?	lema 'anta fii el-bayt?	لِمَ أنت في البيت؟
Why are you here?	lemaThaa 'anta hunaa?	لِماذا أنت هنا؟
Where is the book?	'ayn al-ketaab?	أين الكتاب؟
Who is he?	man huwa?	مَن هو؟
When is the lesson?	mataa ad-dars	مَتى الدرس؟
How do you say?	kayf taquul?	كيف تَقول؟
Are you an Arab?	hal 'anta Aarabyy?	هل أنت عربي؟
Where are you from?	men 'ayn 'anta?	مِنْ أين أنت؟
Which book is this?	'ayy ketaab haThaa?	أي كتاب هذا؟

Say it in Arabic

1- What is your name?

2- What do you do?

3- Why are you at home today?

4- Where is the message?

5- Who is she?

6- When is the lesson?

7- How do you say?

8- Are you in the office?

9- Where are you from?

10- Which street is this?

Exercise 1: Match each question in **A** with an appropriate answer in **B**

B	
esmii Sarah	اِسْمي سارة
'anaa meSryy	أنا مِصْريّ
'anaa amriiky-ya	أنا أمريكيّة
esmii 'adam	اِسْمي آدم
bekhayr	بخَير

A	
maa esmuka?	مَا اِسْمُك؟
men 'ayn 'anti?	مِن أَيْنَ أنْتِ؟
men 'ayn 'anta?	مِن أَيْنَ أنْتَ؟
maa esmuke?	مَا اِسْمُكِ؟
kayf al-Haal?	كَيْف الحال؟

Exercise 2: What does it mean?

English	Transliteration	Arabic
…………………………	*maa esmuk?*	1- ما اِسْمُك؟
…………………………	*matha taAmal?*	2- ماذا تَعْمَل؟
…………………………	*lema 'anta fii meSr?*	3- لِمَ أنتَ في مِصْر؟
…………………………	*'ayn al-jaameAa ?*	4- أيْن الجامِعَة؟
…………………………	*man 'adam?*	5- مَنْ آدَم؟
…………………………	*mataa ad-dars?*	6- مَتى الدّرْس؟.
…………………………	*hal 'anta men Faransaa?*	8- هل أنْتَ مِنْ فَرَنْسا؟
…………………………	*men 'ayn 'anta?*	9-من أين أنت؟
…………………………	*men 'ayy balad 'anta?*	10- مِنْ أَي بَلَد أنتَ ؟

Exercise 3: Identify the nationality of the following countries.

Female nationality	Male nationality	Country	
……………………..	……………………	كندا kanada	
……………………..	……………………	أمريكا amriika	
……………………..	……………………	بريطانيا briiTanya	

....   اليابان

al-yaabaan

....   اوستراليا

ostoraalyaa

Exercise 4: Identify the nationality of the following personal pronouns.

The country name is given in the brackets:

1.*huwa*…………............ . (*meSr*)   هو..................... .(مصر).1

2.*heya*……................. (*amriikaa*)   هي..................... (أمريكا).2

3.*hal 'anta* …...........? (*al-hind*= India)   3. هل أنْتَ .... ؟ (الهند)

4. *hal 'anti*…………...........? (*fransaa*)   4.هَلْ أنْتِ .... ؟(فرنسا)

5.*'anaa* ………...............(*al-Aeraaq*)   5.أنا.....................(العراق)

Exercise 5: Find out three Arab countries on the map and your country and write them in Arabic below.

.... 3-   1-

.... 4-   2-

Exercise 6: Using the words below, fill in the puzzle with the country name.

Down   Across

4- مغرب   1- مصر

5- يمن   2- كويت

           3- قطر

		4-1				
					5	2
			3			

Exercise 7: Can you find the four Arabic meanings for the words below in the word square?

1- City

2- School

3- University

4- Message

5- House

ظ	ة	ن	ي	د	م	ر
ذ	ز	ة	س	ر	د	م
ة	ع	م	ا	ج	خ	ح
ي	ة	ل	ا	س	ر	و
ض	ص	ق	ت	ي	ب	ط

Exercise 8: Match the picture with the meaning.

غُرْفَة

ghurfa

بَيْت

bayt

قَلَم

qalam

كِتاب

Ketaab

مَكْتَب

maktab

كُرْسِي

kursy

Exercise 9: Translate into Arabic.

1- Where are you from?

....

2-What is your name?

....

3- Are you Emirati? (Males and females)

....

4- What do you do?

....

5- Nice to meet you.

....

6- Which country are you from?

....

7- When is the lesson?

....

8- Who is he / she?

....

9- Who are they?

....

10- Why are you in Egypt?

....

11- Where is the school?

....

12- Where are you? (Male / Female / Plural)

....

Learn these prepositions

English	Transliteration	Arabic
on	Aala	عَلَى
by / in / at	be	بـ
with	maAa	مَع
to	ilaa	إلَى
for / to	le	لـ
about	Aan	عَن

Visit the book website to find out more!
http://www.LetsTalkArabic.com

Vocabulary

اِسْم
esm,name

اِسْمي
esmii,my name

ما اِسْمُكَ؟
maa esmuk?,what's your name?

اِسْمُكَ
esmuka,your name(for male)

اِسْمُكِ
esmuke,your name(for female)

مِنْ فَضْلِكِ
men faDlek,please

لَوْ سَمَحْت
law samaHt,if you would

بَلَد
balad,country

عَرَبي
Aarabyy,Arab

مِنْ
men,from

أَيْن؟
'ayn,where?

مِن أَيْن؟
men ayn,from where?

أَمْريكيّ
'amriikyy,American

مِصْريّ
meSryy,Egyptian

فُرْصَة سَعيدَة

حاسِب
Haaseb,computer

مَقْعَد
meqAad,seat

غُرْفَة
ghurfa,room

بَيْت
bayt,home

فَصْل
faSl,classroom

مَدْرَسَة
madrasa,school

جامِعَة
jameAa,university

كُلّيّة
kul-ley-ya,college/ faculty

مَدينة
madiina,city/ town

رِسَالة
resaala,message

مِنْطقة
menTaqa,area / region

هُنَا
hunaa,here

هُنَاك
hunaak,there

أنا
'anaa,I

نَحْنُ

46

furSa saAiida,Nice to meet you

تَشَرَّفْنا

tashar-rafna,Honored to meet you.

عُنوان

Aunwaan,address

هَذا

haThaa,this

كُرسي

kursii,chair

كِتَاب

ketaab,book

مَكْتَب

maktab,office/ desk

طَاوِلة

Taawela,table

ماذا؟

maaThaa,What? (used before verbs)

لِمَ / لِماذا؟

lema / lemaaThaa,Why?

مَنْ؟

man,Who?

مَتَى؟

mataa,When?

كَيْف؟

kayf,How?

هلْ؟

hal,For (Yes/No) question

مَعَ مَنْ؟

maAa man,With whom?

أي؟

'ayy,Which?

بِـ

be,by / in / at

لِـ

le,for / to

إِلَى

ilaa,to

مَعَ

maAa,with

عَلَى

Aalaa,on

في

fii,in / at

naHnu,We

أَنتَ

'anta,You (for male)

أَنْتِ

'anti,You (for female)

أَنتُم

'antum,You (plural)

هُوَ

huwa,He / It (for masculine)

هِيَ

heya,She /It (for feminine)

هُم

hum,They (plural)

ما؟

maa,What? (used before nouns)

UNIT THREE

What is this?

UNIT THREE

What is this?

Contents

- Demonstratives

- Useful adjectives

- Grammar and usage

- Simple sentences

- Noun-Adjective phrases

- Exercises

What's this?
maa haThaa / haThehe?
ما هَذا / هَذِهِ؟

Demonstratives

The demonstratives *"haTha / haThehe"* are the two used words to point in the phrases like "this is a/an…." and "this…"

Look at the below examples and learn how to say "this is a" & "this is the":

1- **This is a / an**… (Pointing to a masculine)

هَذا قَلَم
haThaa qalam
This is a pen

هَذا كِتاب
haThaa Ketaab
This is a book

هَذا بَيْت
haThaa bayt
This is a house

هَذا هَاتِف
haThaa haatef
This is a telephone

هَذا مَكْتَب
haThaa maktab
This is an office / desk

هَذا كُرْسي
haThaa kursy
This is a chair

2- This is a / an…(Pointing to a feminine)

هَذِهِ سَيّارَة
haThehe say-yaara
This is a car

هَذِهِ غُرْفَة
haThehe ghurfa
This is a room

هَذِهِ بِنْت
haThehe bent
This is a girl

هَذِهِ صُورَة
haThehe Suura
This is a picture

هَذِهِ ساعَة
haThehe saaAa
This is a watch

هَذِهِ مَكْتَبة
haThehe maktaba
This is a library

3- This… (Pointing to a masculine)

هَذا القَلَم
haThaa al-qalam
This pen

هَذا الكِتاب
haThaa al-ketaab
This book

هَذا البَيْت
haThaa al-bayt
This house

هَذا الهَاتِف
haTha al-haatef
This telephone

هَذا المَكْتَب
haTha al-maktab
This office / desk

هَذا الكُرْسي
haTha al-kursy
This chair

4- **This**... (Pointing to a feminine)

هَذِهِ السَّيّارَة
haThehe es-say-yaara
This car

هَذِهِ الغُرْفَة
haThehe el-ghurfa
This room

هَذِهِ البِنْت
haThehe el-bent
This girl

هَذِهِ الصُّورَة
haThehe eS-Suura
This picture

هَذِهِ السّاعَة
haThehe es-saaAa
This watch

هَذِهِ الطّاوِلَة
haThehe eT-Taawela
This table

Useful adjectives:

(m) is abbreviation for (masculine) & (f) is abbreviation for (feminine). You can see that the basic rule in the Arabic language is to put "ة" "*taa marbuuta*" to the masculine noun or adjective to make it feminine.

English	Transliteration	Arabic
big /(old for human)	*kabiir (m)*	كَبير
	kabiira (f)	كَبيرة
small	*Saghiir (m)*	صَغير
	Saghiira(f)	صَغيرة

far	*baAiid (m)*	بَعيد
	baAiida (f)	بَعيدة
near / close to	*qariib (m)*	قَريب
	qariiba (f)	قَريبة

old (not for human)	qadiim (m)	قَديم
	qadiima (f)	قَديمة
new	jadiid (m)	جَديد
	jadiida (f)	جَديدة
good	jay-yed (m)	جَيِّد
	jay-yeda (f)	جَيِّدة
bad	say-ye' (m)	سَيِّء
	say-ye'a (f)	سَيِّئة
wide	waaseA (m)	واسِعْ
	waaseAa (f)	واسِعَة
narrow	Day-yeq (m)	ضَيِّق
	Day-yeqa (f)	ضَيِّقة
beautiful	jamiil (m)	جَميل
	jamiila (f)	جَميلة
	makruuh (m)	مَكْروه
ugly	makruuha (f)	مَكروهة
nice	laTiif (m)	لَطيف
	laTiifa (f)	لَطيفة

long / tall	*Tawiil (m)*	طَويل
	Tawiila (f)	طَويلة
short	*qaSiir (m)*	قَصير
	qaSiira (f)	قَصيرة
strong	*qawy*	قوي
	qawy-ya	قوية
	DaAiif	ضعيف
weak	*DaAiifa*	ضعيفة
kind	*Tay-yeb (m)*	طيب
	tay-yeba (f)	طَيَبة
hard	*SaAb (m)*	صَعب
	SaAba (f)	صَعبة
easy	*sahl (m)*	سَهل
	sahla (f)	سهلة

Examples:

Transliteration	**Arabic**
ar-rajul kabiir	الرجل كبير
al-walad Saghiir	الولد صغير

al-bayt baaiid	البيت بعيد
as-say-yara qariiba	السيارة قريبة
al-haatef qadiim	الهاتف قديم
al-madrasa jadiida	المدرسة جديدة
al-bent jay-yeda	البنت جَيّدة
al-walad say-ye'	الولد سيء
ash-shaare' waasA	الشارع واسع
ash-shaare' Day-yeq	الشارع ضيق
almar'a jamiila	المرأة جميلة
al-bent laTiifa	البنت لطيفة
Adam Tawiil	آدم طويل
Sara qaSiira	سارة قصيرة
rajul Tay-yeb	رجل طيب
yawm SaAb	يوم صعب
al-Aaraby-ya sahla	العربية سهلة

Learn this word:

جداً *jed-dan* = very & so

Say it in Arabic

1- The office is very wide

2- The house is far

3- This is a very nice day

4- This is a beautiful girl

5- The phone old

6- Cairo is a big city

7- This is a long street

8- The car is new

9- He is so kind

10- she is so nice

Grammar notice

1- Simple Sentences

Many Arabic sentences do not need the verb "to be" (am, is, are) in the present tense, which means that you can have a (nominal sentence) without verbs at all. Look at the below phrases;

أنا مُهَنْدِس	أنا مِنْ سوريا	أنا أحْمَد
'anaa muhandes	*'anaa men suurya*	*'anaa 'aHmad.*
I (am) an engineer	I (am) from Syria	I (am) Ahmad.
هُوَ مُحاسِب	هُوَ مِنْ قَطِر	هُوِ حَمْدان
huwa muHaaseb	*huwa men qatar*	*huwa Hamdaan*
He (is) an accountant	He (is) from Qatar	He (is) Hamdan
هُمْ مِن جَدّة	أنتُّم مِن دُبَي	نَحْنُ مِن الإمارات
hum men jad-da	*'antum men dubai*	*naHnu men al-emaaraat*
They (are) from Jeddah	You (are) all from Dubai	We (are) from Emirates
المَدينَة كَبيرَة	الجَوّ لَطيف	البَيْت جَميل
al-madiina kabiira	*al-jaww laTiif*	*al-bayt jamiil*
The city (is) big	The weather (is) nice	The house (is) beautiful

2- Noun-Adjective phrases

It is simple to form an adjective phrase in Arabic, because **the adjective follows the noun**, as in the below example.

بَيْت كَبير

bayt kabiir

a big house

البَيْت الكَبير

al-bayt al-kabiir

the big house

As you can see in the two examples, if the noun has a definite article (*al*), the adjective must be with *al*, and vice versa.

Remember that if the first word or noun is definite or with the article *"al"* and the second word is not definite, it will be considered a full nominal sentence, as in the grammar notice number 1. For example,

البَيْت كَبير

al-bayt kabiir

The house **is** big

3- The Plural *al-jamA* الجَمْع

Arabic has three types of plurals:

1- Masculine Plural	*jamA el-muThak-kar*	1-جَمْع المُذَكّر
2- Feminine Plural	*jamA el-mu'an-nath*	2-جَمْع المُؤنّث
3- Broken Plural	*jamA et-taksiir*	3-جَمْع التكسير

1- Masculine plural

The noun takes one of pair endings (either "*uun*"و‍ـــــــ – or "*iin*"ي‍ـــــــن) according to grammatical function, which you will learn in the intermediate levels. While in spoken Arabic they use only one of the above suffixes, which is "*iin*".

For example:

English	plural	Singular
Egyptian/ Egyptians	مِصْريون / مِصريين *meSryuun / meSryiin*	مِصْري *meSryy*
Emirati / Emiratis	إماراتيون / إماراتيين *'emaraatyuun/ 'emaraatyiin*	إماراتي *'emaraatyy*
Qatari / Qataris	قَطَريون / قَطَريين *qataryuun / qataryiin*	قَطَري *qataryy*
Kuwaiti / Kuwaitis	كويتيون / كويتيين *kuwaityuun / kuwaityiin*	كُويتي *kuwaityy*
Teacher / Teachers	مُدَرّسون / مُدَرّسين *mudar-resuun/ mudar-resiin*	مُدَرّس *mudar-res*
Manager / Managers	مُديرون / مُديرين *mudiiruun / mudiiriin*	مُدير *mudiir*

Exercise 1: Listen to unit three audio online and write down what you hear. The website is: www.LetsTalkArabic.com

....

....

Exercise 2: Translate into Arabic

1- The house is wide.

…………………………………………………………………………..

2- The city is beautiful.

…………………………………………………………………………..

3- This is an office.

…………………………………………………………………………..

4- This chair is small.

…………………………………………………………………………..

5- This table is long.

…………………………………………………………………………..

6- This is an old school.

…………………………………………………………………………..

7- Hamdan is Qatari and Ahmad is Emirati.

…………………………………………………………………………..

8- They are from Kuwait.

…………………………………………………………………………..

9- This is a new book.

…………………………………………………………………………..

10- This is a tall girl, and this is a small boy.

…………………………………………………………………………..

11- This is a nice day.

…………………………………………………………………………..

12- The new university is big.

…………………………………………………………………………..

Exercise 3: Translate into English

Transliteration	Arabic
1- al-bayt Saghiir.	١- البَيْت صَغير.
....	....
2- haThehe el-madiina qadiima.	٢- هَذِه المَدينَة قَديمَة.
....	....
3- haTha maktab waaseA.	٣- هذا مَكْتَب واسِع.
....	....
4- haThehe madrasa.	٤- هذِه مَدْرَسة.
....	....
5- 'adam men madiinat el-qaahera.	٥- آدَم مِن مَدينَة القاهِرة.
....	....
6- saara Aeraaqy-ya, men al-baSra.	٦- سارة عِراقية؛ مِن البَصْرَة.
....	....
7- hum men madiinat 'abu THabii.	٧- هُمْ مِن مَدينة أبوظبي.
....	....
8- haTha ketaab jay-yed.	٨- هذا كِتاب جيّد.
....	....

Exercise 4: What is this? Write below the picture.

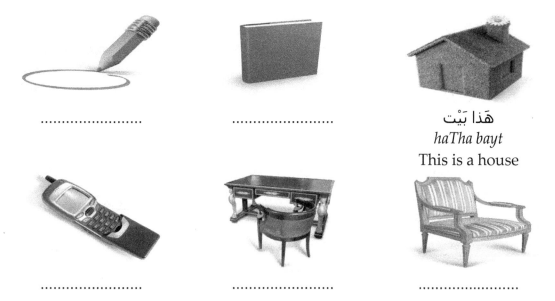

....   هَذا بَيْت
haTha bayt
This is a house

....

Exercise 5: Combine the following pairs of words to make a useful nominal sentence or noun-adjective phrase as in number one.

Transliteration	Arabic
1- jaameAa / baAiida	١- جامِعَة / بَعيدة
al-jaameAa baAiida.	الجَامِعَة بَعيدَة
2- *ghurfa / jadiida*	٢- غُرْفَة / جديدة
....	....
3- *Hasuub / qadiim*	٣- حاسـوب / قَديم
....	....
4- *resaala / Taweela*	٤- رِسـالَة / طَويلَة
....	....
5- *madiina / jamiila*	٥- مَدينة / جَميلة
....	....

Exercise 6: Match the picture with the meaning.

غُرْفة

ghurfa

بِنْت

bent

مَكْتَبة

maktaba

ساعَة

saaAa

مَكْتَب

maktab

سَيّارَة

say-yaara

Exercise 7: Match the balloon with the meaning

good

bad

wide

narrow

nice

old

new

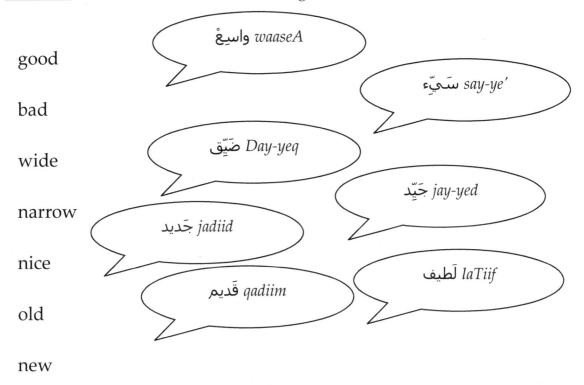

واسِعْ waaseA

سَيِّء say-ye'

ضَيّق Day-yeq

جَيِّد jay-yed

جَديد jadiid

لَطيف laTiif

قَديم qadiim

Exercise 8: Can you find the four Arabic meanings for the words below in the word square?

1- Tall

2- Beautiful

3- Small

4- Big

5- Old

ي	ط	و	ي	ل	ة	ر
ج	م	ي	ل	ه	ح	ز
ك	ص	غ	ي	ر	ث	ى
س	ش	ك	ب	ي	ر	ف
ق	د	ي	م	ت	ن	و

Exercise 9: Describe these nouns as in the first example:

1- *haTha maktab **waaseA**.*	١- هذا مَكْتَب **واسِع**
2- *haThehe madrasa* ………………..	٢- هذِهِ مَدْرَسة …………………
3- *Adam* …………….	٣- آدَم ……………………
4- *Sara* ………………	٤- سـارة ……………………
5- *madiinat 'abu THabii* ………………	٥- مَدينة أبوظبي ……………
6- *haThehe el-madiina* …………………	٦- هَذِه المَدينَة ………………
7- *madiinat el-qaahera* …………………	٧- مَدينَة القاهِرة ……………
8- *haTha ketaab* ……………………	٨- هذا كِتاب ……………

Exercise 10: Using the words below, fill in the puzzle with the Arabic adjectives. Remember to go from right to left or up to down.

Down	Across
3- big	1- small
4- old	2- new

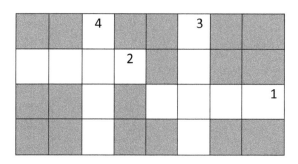

Vocabulary

What's this?	ما هَذا؟	maa haThaa
This is a house	هَذا بَيْت	haThaa bayt
This is a book	هَذا كِتاب	haThaa Ketaab
This is a pen	هَذا قَلَم	haThaa qalam
This is a chair	هَذا كُرْسِي	haThaa kursy
This is an office / desk	هَذا مَكْتَب	haThaa maktab
This is a telephone	هَذا هَاتِف	haThaa haatef
This is a girl	هَذِهِ بِنْت	haThehe bent
This is a room	هَذِهِ غُرْفَة	haThehe ghurfa
This is a car	هَذِهِ سَيَّارَة	haThehe say-yaara
This is a library	هَذِهِ مَكْتَبَة	haThehe maktaba
This is a watch	هَذِهِ ساعَة	haThehe saaAa
This is a picture	هَذِهِ صُورَة	haThehe Suura
big	كبير	kabiir
small	صَغير	Saghiir
far	بَعيد	baAiid
near	قَريب	qariib
old	قَديم	qadiim
new	جَديد	jadiid
good	جَيِّد	jay-yed
bad	سَيِّء	say-ye'
wide	واسِع	waaseA
narrow	ضَيَّق	Day-yeq
beautiful	جَميل	jamiil
nice	لَطيف	laTiif
long / tall	طَويل	Tawiil
short	قَصير	qaSiir
good / Kind	طيب	Tay-yeb
easy	سَهل	sahl
hard	صَعب	SaAb
very	جِدًّا	jed-dan

Visit the book website to find out more!
http://www.LetsTalkArabic.com

UNIT FOUR

The family

UNIT FOUR

The family

Contents

- The family

- Vocabulary

- Culture notes

- Vocabulary practices

- Grammar usage: possessive pronouns

- Exercises

The Family

al-Aaa'ela العائِلَة

Dialogue:

English	Transliteration	Arabic
Adam: Welcome Majed.	*A: marHaban maajed.*	آدَم: مَرْحَباً ماجِد.
Majed: Hello Adam.	*B: 'ahlan Adam.*	ماجِد:أهْلاَ آدَم.
Adam: It seems you are busy!	*A: 'anta mashghuul!*	آدَم:أنتَ مَشْغول!
Majed: No, this is my brother Ayman. He is a student also here at the university.	*B: laa haTHaa 'akhii 'ayman. huwa Taalib hunaa fii al-jaameAa 'ayDan.*	ماجِد:لا,هَذِا أخْي أيمن. هُوَ طالِب هُنا في الجامِعَة أَيْضاً.
Adam: Really! Welcome Ayman!	*A: feAlan?! marHaban 'ayman!*	آدَم: فِعْلا؟! مَرْحَبا أيمنْ.
Ayman: Hi Adam.	*B: 'ahlan wa sahlan 'adam*	أيمن:أهْلاَ وَسَهْلا آدَم.
Adam: I have a brother. He also studies at the same university.	*A: wa 'anaa 'ayDan lii 'akh yadrus fii nafs el-jaamiAa*	آدَم: وأنا أيْضَا لي أخ يَدْرُس في نَفْس الجامِعَة.
Ayman: Nice to meet you.	*C: fursa saAiida jid-dan*	أيمن : قُرْصة سعيدة جِدّاً.
Adam: Nice to meet you too.	*A: tashar-rafna*	آدَم: تَشَرّفْنا.

Vocabulary followed by unhighlighted sentences as an example

English	Transliteration	Arabic
extended family	*Aa'ela*	عائِلة
immediate family	*usra*	أُسْرَة
I have	*lii*	لي

lii usra Saghiira		لي أُسرة صغيرة
lii Aa'ela kabiira jed-dan		لي عائلة كبيرة جِدّاً
father	*'abb / waaled*	أبّ / والِد
waaled Adam rajul Tay-yeb		والِد آدم رجل طيب
mother	*umm / waaleda*	أمٌّ / والِدَة
umm Ali meSry-ya		أمّ عَلي مِصرية
sister	*ukht*	أُخْت
brother	*'akh*	أخْ
ukht Sara bent laTiifa		أخت سارة بنت لطيفة
lii 'akh Saghiir		لي أخ صغير
son	*ebn*	اِبْن
lii ebn 'akh jamiil		لي اِبن أخ جميل
grandfather	*jadd*	جَدّ
grandmother	*jad-da*	جَدّة
jad-dy rajul kabiir		جدّي رَجُل كبير
jad-dat Adam emra'a laTiifa		جدة آدم اِمرأة لطيفة
boy	*walad*	وَلَد
girl / daughter	*bent*	بِنْت
huwa walad say-ye'		هو ولد سيِّء

heya bent jamiila		هي بنت جميلة
busy	mashghuul /mashghula	مَشْغول / مَشْغُولة
really, truly	feA'lan	فِعلاً
'anaa feA'lan mashghuul		أنا فعلا مشغول
friend	Sadiiq / Sadiiqa	صَديق / صَديقَة
aHmad Sadiiq jay-yed		أحمد صديق جيد
student	Taaleb / Taaleba	طالِب / طالِبَة
sara Taaliba		سارة طالبة
here	hunaa	هُنا
baytii hunaa		بيتي هُنا
there	hunaak	هُناك
al-maktab hunaak		المكتب هناك
same	nafs	نَفْس
'anaa wa Adam fii nafs al-jaame'a		أنا وآدم في نفس الجامعة
also, as well	kamaa 'an / 'ayDan	كَما أَن / أَيْضاْ
'anaa 'ayDan mashghuul		أنا أيضا مشغول
I study	'adrus	أدْرُس
language	lugha	لُغة
'adrus lugha Aaraby-ya		أدْرُس لغة عربية

he studies	*yadrus*	يَدْرُس
'akhii yadrus al-faransy-ya		أخي يدرُس الفرنسية
she studies	*tadrus*	تَدرُس
ukhtii tadrus al-almaany-ya		أختي تَدرُس الألمانية
husband	*zawj*	زَوج
wife	*zawja*	زَوجة
paternal uncle / aunt	*Am / Am-ma*	عَم / عَمّة
maternal uncle / aunt	*khaal / khaala*	خال / خالة
zawjat Am-mii Tawiila wa jamiila		زوجة عمي طويلة وجَميلة
married	*mutazaw-wej / a*	مُتَزَوّج / مُتَزَوّجة
hal 'anta mutazaw-wej? nAam		هل أنتَ مُتزوج؟ نعم

Say it in Arabic

1- I have a small family, I, my father and my mother

2- I have a nice sister

3- My mother is a teacher in the university

4- I have a beautiful daughter and a nice son

5- I'm a student and my friend is a teacher

6- I'm really busy this evening

7- Are you busy today as well?

8- I study in the same university with my sister

9- Are you married? (male/female)

Culture Notes

Arabs usually assume that the family values have to be shared among all members of the society in general. The extended family plays a more important role in Arab society than it does in Western society. Family members visit each other often as well as on social occasions if they live in the same city. However, many people also feel that this general habit has decreased in recent years.

Grammar usage

Possessive pronouns

Possessive pronouns in Arabic are suffixes attached to the nouns. Those you have seen already in previous dialogues:

my name : *esmii* اِسْمِي   my brother: *akhii* أخي

your name: *esmka / esmke* اِسْمَكَ / اِسْمَكِ

Here are all these suffixes with their subject pronouns, applied on an example:

English	Transliteration	Arabic		
my office	*maktabii*	مَكْتَبِـي	First	person
our office	*maktabnaa*	مَكْتَبـنا		
your office (for a male)	*maktabka / ak* (spoken)	مَكْتَبـكَ	Second	person
your office (for a female)	*maktabke / ek* (spoken)	مَكْتَبـكِ		
your office (for plural)	*maktabkum*	مَكْتَبـكُم		
his office	*maktabhu*	مَكْتَبـهُ	Third	person
her office	*maktabhaa*	مَكْتَبـها		
their office	*maktabhum*	مَكْتَبـهُم		

Notice that, the possessive pronouns (*ka*) and (*ke*) for your are pronounced as (*ak*) for male and (*ek*) for female in spoken Arabic.

EXAMPLES

esmii Adam, haThaa baytii	اسمي آدم؛ هذا بيتي
maktabnaa hunaa, wa baytnaa hunaak	مكتبنا هنا؛ وبيتنا هناك
hal haThaa maktabuka?	هل هذا مكتبك؟
maa esmuke?	ما اسمك؟
hal haThaa baytkum?	هل هذا بيتكم؟
esmuhu Ahmad,wa haThaa bayt-hu	اسمُه أحمد؛ وهذا بيتُه
esmuhaa Sara, wa haThaa bayt-haa	اسمها سارة؛ وهذا بيتها
bayt-hum bAiid, wa maktabhum jadiid	بيتهم بعيد؛ مكتبهم جديد

Say it in Arabic

1- My name is .. and this is my brother

2- Our house is there, our city is beautiful

3- What is your name?

4- Is this your book?

5- Is this your office guys?

6- His name is Ahmad. his house is in Cairo and his family is in Qatar

7- Her name is Mary, her daughter is nice

 8- Their car is big, their house is wide

Fill in the blanks with one of the new words

1- .... usra Saghiira, 'anaa, wa 'abii, wa um-mii.

2- lii .... kabiira jed-dan.

3- lii 'akh Saghiir, wa huwa yadrus fii .... al-kul-ly-ya.

4- 'anaa feA'lan .... alyawm fii el-maktab.

5- Sadiiqii .... al-espaany-ya.

6- .... al-Araby-ya fii jaameAt al-qaahera.

7- lii ukht Saghiira, wa heya .... fii haThehe el-madrasa.

8- 'ahlan, 'anaa Taaleb hunaa fii haThehe eljaame'A, hal 'anta Taaleb ....?

1- .... أسرة صغيرة؛ أنا؛ وأبي؛ وأمي.

2- لي .... كبيرة جدا.

3- لي أخ صغير؛ وهو يدرس في .... الكلية.

4- أنا فِعلا .... اليوم في المكتب.

5- صديق .... الإسبانية.

6- .... العربية في جامعة القاهرة.

7- لي أخت صغيرة؛ وهي .... في هذه المدرسة.

8- أهلا؛ أنا طالب هنا في هذه الجامعة. هل أنت طالب ....؟

Exercise 1: Translate into Arabic

1- What is this?

....

2- I'm here, he is here.

....

3- I'm really busy today.

....

4- Are you busy as well?

....

5- She is very happy.

....

6- I have a brother and he studies Arabic.

....

7- He is an engineer at the same office.

....

8- He studies Arabic at the American University.

....

9- I'm busy with a friend.

....

Exercise 2: Translate into English

1- suzaan Taaleba fii el-jaameAa.

١- سوزان طالِبة في الجامِعَة.

....

....

2- haThehe ukhtii saara.

٢- هَذِه أُخْتي سارَة.

....

....

3- 'akhii mashghuul fii el-maktab.

٣- أخي مَشغول في المَكْتَب.

....

....

4- heya Taaleba fii nafs el-kul-ly-ya.

٤- هِيَ طالْبَة في نَفس الكلّية.

....

....

5- John yadrus al-Aaraby-ya.

٥- جون يَدرُس العَرَبِيّة.

....

....

Exercise 3: Circle every member of the family in the words below

أخْت	مَكْتَب	جَدّ	أمّ
ukht	maktab	jadd	umm
الكلّية	كِتاب	أخْ	أبْ
al-kul-ly-ya	ketaab	'akh	'ab
خَال	جَدّة	إبْن	إبْنة
khaal	jad-da	ebn	ebna

Exercise 4: Practice using subject pronouns, as in the example number one as it is already answered:

Transliteration	Arabic

*1- hal **anta** meSryy*

1- هَلْ **أَنْتَ** مِصْري؟

*naAam **anaa** meSryy*

نعم؛ **أنا** مِصْري.

2- men 'ayn .... yaa 'adam?

2- مِن أَيْنَ .... يا آدم؟

............men dubai.

.... مِنْ دُبَي.

3-hal .... faransy-ya ya Sara?

3-هل .... فَرَنْسية يا سارة؟

laa........... 'amriiky-ya.

لا .... أمريكية

4- man suzan? -------khaalat sara

4- مَنْ سوزان؟ .... خالة سارة

5- 'ayn Adam?

5- أَيْنَ آدم؟

.... fii meSr

.... في مِصْر.

Exercise 5: Complete The Arabic cross word puzzle! Write down the Arabic meaning for the words below.

Down	Cross
1- Busy	3- Really
2- Same	

Exercise 6: Practice using possessive pronouns, as in the example number one as it is already answered.

Example: *(maa esm / 'anta)? Maa **esmuka**?* ما (اسم / أنتَ)؟ ما **اسمُكَ**؟

Transliteration	Arabic
1- *'ayn (bayt/antum)?*	1-أين(بَيْت/أنتم)؟
2- *hal (Sadiiq/'anta) Taalib?*	2-هَلْ(صَديق/أنتَ) طالِب؟
3- *hya amriiky-ya wa (usra/hya) fii Canada.*	3-هي أمريكية و(أسْرة/هي) في كَنَدا.
4- *(kuly-ya/huwa) fii dubai.*	4-(كلية/هو)في دبي.
5- *(bayt/nHnu) fii al-qaahera.*	5-(بيت/نحن) في القاهرة.
6- *hal (ketaab/'anti) jadiid?*	6-هل(كِتاب/أنتِ)جَديد؟
7- *'ayn(maktab/'antum)?*	7-أين (مَكْتَبْ/أنتم)؟
8- *hal(jaameAa/'antum) qadiima?*	8-هل(جامعة/أنتم) قديمة؟
9- *(ebn/'anaa) (esm /huwa) khalid*	9-(إبن/أنا) (اسم / هو) خالد.

Exercise 7: Can you find four words you have learned in the word square? Write out the meanings of the words you have found as in the example.

1- **Busy**......................

2- ....

3- ....

4- ....

5- ....

م	ش	غ	و	ل	ن	ه
ز	ة	ا	ل	ن	ف	س
و	هـ	ن	ا	ص	ى	ش
ج	ط	ا	ل	ب	ع	ث
ه	ن	ا	ك	ظ	د	ذ

Exercise 8: Fill in the blanks using the vocabulary you have learned, to make a dialogue.

English	Transliteration	Arabic
Adam: Welcome Maged.	*A: marHaban maajed.*	آدَم: مَرْحَباً ماجِد.
Majed: Hello Adam.	*B: 'ahlan Adam.*	ماجِد:أهْلاً آدَم.
Adam: Are you busy!	*A: ....!*	آدَم:....................!
Majed: No, this is my brother Ayman. He is a student here at the university also.	*B: laa haTHaa 'akhii 'ayman. huwa Taalib hunaa fii al-jaameAa 'ayDan.*	ماجِد:لا,هَذِا أخْي أيمن. هُوَ طالِب هُنا في الجامِعَة أَيْضاً.
Adam: Really! Welcome Ayman!	*A: ....!*	آدم: ....؟! مَرْحَبا أيمنْ.
Ayman: Hi Adam.	*C: 'ahlan wa sahlan 'adam*	أيمن:أهْلاً وَسَهْلا آدَم.
Adam: I have a brother. He also studies at the same university.	*A: ....*	آدم: ....
Ayman: Nice to meet you.	*C: ....*	أيمن : ....
Adam: Nice to meet you too.	*A: tashar-rafna*	آدَم: ....

Exercise 9: Choose the correct Arabic meanings for the English words below

A- Immediate family

3- أُسْرَة	2- عائِلة	1- اِبْنَة
usra	Aa'ela	ebna

B- Extended family

3- أُسْرَة	2- اِبْنَة	1- عائِلة
usra	ebna	Aa'ela

C- Brother

3- جَدّ	2- أخْ	1- أُخْت
jadd	'akh	ukht

D- Siste

3- أخْ	2- أُخْت	1- اِبْنَة
'akh	ukht	ebna

E- Busy

3- مَشْغول	2- وَلَد	1- جَدّ
mashghuul	walad	jadd

F- Same

3- لي	2- كَما أَن	1- نَفْس
lii	kamaa 'an	nafs

G- Also

3- لي	2- كَما أَن	1- نَفْس
lii	Kamaa 'an	nafs

Exercise 10: Put the words in the correct order to make a phrase or sentence. Don't forget to go from right to left.

أخْي	هُوَ	هَذِا	طالِب	1-
'akhii	huwa	haTHaa	Taalib

....

لي أخ	الجامِعَة	نَفْس	يَدْرُس في	2-
lii 'akh	el-jaamiAa	nafs	yadrus fii

....

؟	أنتَ	مَشْغول		3-
	'anta	mashghuul

....

هُوَ	يَدْرُس في	الجامِعَة	هُنا	4-
huwa	yadrus fii	el-jaamiAa	hunaa

....

VOCABULARY

لي
lii,I have

عائِلَة
Aa'ela,extended family

أُسْرَة
usra,immediate family

أبّ
'ab,father

والِد
waaled,father (formal)

أُمّ

هُنا
hunaa,here

هُناك
hunaak,there

نَفْس
nafs,same

فِعْلا
feAlan,really

أيْضاً
'ayDan,also

كما أن

umm,mother
والِدة
waaleda,mother (formal)
أخ
'akh,brother
أُخْت
ukht,sister
اِبْن
ebn,son
جَدّ
jadd,grandfather
جَدَّة
jad-da,grandmother
وَلَد
walad,boy
بِنْت
bent,girl /daughter
زَوج
zawj,husband
زَوجة
zawja,wife
مَشْغول / مَشْغولة
mashghuul /mashghula,busy (male/female)
صَديق / صَديقة
Sadiiq / Sadiiqa,friend (male/female)
طالِب / طالِبة
Taaleb / Taaleba,student (male/female)

kamaa 'an,as well
أدْرُس
'adrus,I study
يَدْرُس
yadrus,he studies
تَدرُس
tadrus,she studies
عَم
Aamm,paternal uncle
عَمّة
Aam-ma,paternal aunt
خال
khaal,maternal uncle
خالة
khaala,maternal aunt
الناس
an-naas,people
لُغة
lugha,language
مُتَزَوِّج / ـة
mutazaw-wej /a,married

UNIT FIVE

What do you do?

UNIT FIVE

What do you do?

Contents

- Dialogue: What do you do?

- Vocabulary

- Culture notes

- Vocabulary practices

- Grammar usage: *Saying 'to have' in Arabic*
Feminine plural
Broken plural

- Exercises

What do you do?

maaThaa tAmal ؟مَاذَا تَعْمَل

Dialogue: Adam has met Majed once again while he was in a hurry before his lectures at the morning in the AUC (American University in Cairo).

English	Transliteration	Arabic
Majed: Good morning Adam? How are things?	M: SabaaH al-khayr ya 'adam? Kayfa l-Haal?	ماجِد: صَباح الخَيْر يا آدَم؟ كَيْف الحَال؟
Adam: I'm fine. How are you Majed?	A: al-Hamdu lil-lah. wa 'anta kayfa l-Haal ya majed?	آدم: الحَمْدُ لِلَّه؛ وَأنْتَ كَيْفَ الحَالُ يا ماجد؟
Majed: I'm fine, but it seems that you are little exhausted!	M:'ana bekhayr. wa laken yabduu an-naka murhaq qaliilan!	ماجِد: أنَا بخَيْر؛ وَلَكِنْ يَبْدُو أنَّكَ مُرْهَق قَلِيلاً!
Adam: Yes Majed, I'm tired.	A: naAam ya majed. 'anaa taAbaan.	آدم: نَعَمْ يا ماجد؛ أنَا تَعْبَان.
Majed: Sorry Adam! Tired of what?!	M: salaamatk ya adam men maa?!	ماجِد: سَلامتك يا آدَم! مِن ما؟!
Adam: Because of work. I study during the day, and I work in the evening.	A: besabab ash-shughl. fa'anaa 'adrus fii an-nahaar wa 'aAmal fii al-masaa'.	آدَم: بِسبب الشُّغْل؛ فَأنَا أدْرُس في النَّهَار؛ وَأعْمَل في المَساء.
Majed: What do you do?	M: wa mathaa taAmal?	ماجِد: وَمَاذَا تَعْمَل؟
Adam: I'm working at a translation office.	A: 'aAmal bemaktab tarjama.	آدم: أعْمَل بِمَكْتَب تَرْجمَة.
Majed: That's good!	M: haThaa jay-yed!	ماجِد: هَذَا جَيّد!
Adam: Yes. Excuse me Majed. I have a lecture now.	A: naAam, Aafwan majed, baAd iThnek. Aendii muHaaDara al'aan.	آدَم: نَعَم؛ عَفْواً ماجد؛ بَعْد إذْنِك؛ عِنْدِي مُحَاضَرَة الآن.
Majed: Okay Adam, good-bye.	M: tafaD-Dal. maAa s-salaama	ماجِد: تَفَضّل؛ مَعَ السَّلامَة.

Vocabulary followed by unhighlighted sentences as an example

English	Transliteration	Arabic
exhausted	murhaq	مُرْهَق
tired	taAbaan	تَعبان
because of	be-sabab	بِسَبَب
work (noun)	alAamal / ash-shughl	العَمَل/ الشُّغل
'anaa taAbaan jed-dan alyawm besabab ash-shughl		أنا تعبان جدا اليوم بِسَبَب الشغل
al-Aamal fii el-jaameA jay-yed		العَمَل في هَذِهِ الجامِعة جَيّد
it seems	yabduu 'an	يَبْدو أن
yabduu 'an haThaa alyawm Tawiil fii el-maktab		يبدو أن هذا اليوم طويل في المكتب
I work (verb)	'aAmal	أَعْمَل
he works	yaAmal	يَعمل
she works	taAmal	تَعمل
'aAmal ben-nahaar wa 'adrus bel-masaa'		أعمل بالنهار وأدرس بالمساء
now	al'aan	الآن
little	qaliilan	قليلاَ

'anaa mashghuul qaliilan al'aan   أنا مشغول قليلا الآن

translation	tarjama	تَرْجَمَة

'aAmal fii maktab tarjama   أعمَل في مَكتب ترجمة

pardon / excuse me	Aafwan	عَفْوآَ
permission	iThn	إِذْن
excuse me	baAd iThnek	بَعْد إِذْنك
lecture	muHaaDara	مُحاضَرَة
I have	Aendii	عِندي

baAd iThnek, Aendii muHaaDara al'aan   بَعد إذنك؛ عندي محاضرة الآن

God bless you!	Salaamatk	سلامَتك
but	laken	لَكِن
employee	muwaTH-THaf/a	مُوَظّف / ـة
possible to	yumken 'an	يُمْكِن أَن
actually / in fact	fil-Haqiiqa	في الحقيقة

fil-Haqiiqa zawjatii muwaTH-THafa, wa

laken laa taAmal al'aan   في الحقيقة زوجتي مُوَظّفة؛ ولكن لا تعمل الآن

Look at the picture and learn about professions:

N	Transliteration	Arabic	N
1	*tab-baakh*	طّبّاخ	1
2	*rajul 'aAmaal (business man)*	رَجُل أعمال	2
3	*shurTy*	شُرطي	3
4	*Tabiib*	طَبيب	4
5	*muhandes (Engineer)*	مُهَندس	5
6	*muSaw-wer*	مُصَوّر	6
7	*muTreb (singer)*	مُطْرِب	7
8	*musiiqaar*	موسيقار	8
9	*ras-saam*	رَسّام	9
10	*laaAeb*	لاعِب	10

Fill in the blanks with one of the new words

1- ....fin-nahaar, wa 'adrus fil-masaa'

1- .... في النهار؛ وأدرس في المساء.

2- 'adrus................ fil-masaa'.

2- أدرس .... في المساء.

3- Aafwan, hal hunaak maktab .... qariib men hunaa?

3- عفوا؛ هل هناك مكتب .... قريب من هنا؟

4- lii Sadiiq .... fii maktab alAamal.

4- لي صديق .... في مكتب العمل.

5- 'anaa taAbaan jed-dan alyawm .... ash-shughl

5- أنا تعبان جدا اليوم .... الشغل.

6- Aendii .... Tawiila fiS-SabaaH, wa muHaaDara qaSiira fil-masaa'.

6- عندي ....طويلة في الصباح؛ ومحاضرة قصيرة في المساء.

7- maaThaa .... Ahmad? huwa muwaTH-THaf fil-jaameAa

7- ماذا .... أحمد؟ هُوَ مُوظف في الجامعة.

Culture Notes: As in most cultures all over the world, it is common practice in Arabic Culture that when you meet someone who asks you about your condition or who opens any other topic with you, you should ask his or her permission before leaving or finishing the conversation, because it's considered rude to leave in such a way without saying anything. To leave politely, you say, _Aafwan / baAd iThnak/ek._

Grammar usage

Saying (to have) in Arabic

You have noticed Adam in the dialogue when he said (_Aendii muHaaDara_)= I have a lecture. The pronoun forms, which he used with the preposition are basically the same like the possessive pronouns forms which were mentioned in the previous lesson. The following table introduces these endings with prepositions indicating the meaning of (to have) in Arabic.

Saying to have: prepositions with possessive suffixes

English	لِ L		عِنْدَ Aend		مَعَ maAa		
I have	لِي	lii	عِنْدِي	Aendii	مَعِي	maAii	First person
We have	لَنَا	lanaa	عِنْدَنا	Aendnaa	مَعَنَا	maAanaa	
You have (m)	لَكَ	laka	عِنْدَك	Aendka	مَعَك	maAaka	Second person
You have (f)	لَكِ	lake	عِنْدك	Aendke	مَعَك	maAake	
You have (pl)	لَكُم	lakum	عِنْدَكم	Aendkum	مَعَكم	maAakum	
He has	لَه	lahu	عِنْدَه	Aendhu	مَعَه	maAahu	Third person
She has	لَها	lahaa	عِنْدَها	Aendhaa	مَعِها	maAahaa	
They have	لَهُم	lahum	عِنْدَهم	Aendhum	مَعهُم	maAahum	

Three of these combinations form (to have) in Arabic. The difference in how they are used to express possession is:

- (*lii*) is used when referring to owning people: (lii 'akh) = I have a brother
- (*Aend*) is used when referring to owning objects: (Aendii say-yaara) = I have a car
- (*maAa*) is used for referring to owning something right now: (maAii dollar)= I have a dollar. While some Arabic speakers use (*Aend*) for all cases.

Negation of (to have)

You can use (*laysa*"لَيس") to negate (to have) in Arabic, whatever the subject is. See the following examples:

English	Transliteration	Arabic
I don`t have money	*Laysa maAii fuluus*	لَيْسَ مَعي قُلوس
He doesn't have a car	*Laysa Aendahu say-yara*	لَيْسَ عِنْده سَيّارة
They don`t have children	*Laysa lahum awlaad*	لَيْسَ لَهُم أوْلاد

Say it in Arabic

1- I have a brother, his name is Ahmad.

2- We have a house in Cairo.

3- Do you have a car? asking (male,female,group)

4- Do you have work today? asking (male,female,group)

5- Do you have an Arabic book? asking (male,female,group)

6- My husband has a big car.

7- My wife has a very big family.

8- They have a house in this city.

2- Feminine Plural

Most of the nouns which refer to feminine take the ending "aat ات" For example:

English	plural	Singular
Egyptian/ Egyptians (female)	مِصْريات *meSry-yaat*	مِصْرية *meSry-ya*
Emirati / Emiratis (female)	إماراتيات *'emaraaty-yaat*	إماراتية *'emaraaty-ya*
Kuwaiti / Kuwaitis (female)	كويتيات *kuwaity-yaat*	كُويتية *kuwaity-ya*
Teacher / Teachers (female)	مُدَّرِسات *mudar-resaat*	مُدَّرِسة *mudar-resa*
Manager / Managers (female)	مُديرات *mudiiraat*	مُديرة *mudiira*
Car / Cars (Considered feminine)	سَيّارات *say-yaraat*	سَيّارة *say-yaara*
Table / Tables (Considered feminine)	طاوِلات *Taawelaat*	طاوِلَة *Taawela*

3- Broken Plural

Arabic has more than ten patterns of the broken plural which you will learn in intermediate level, as in some English words "child / children, man / men, and woman / women". For example:

English	plural	Singular
Man / Men	رجال *rejaal*	رَجُل *Rajul*
Woman / Women	نساء *nesaa'*	اِمْرأة *'emra'aa*
Child / Children	أطْفال *'aTfaal*	طِفْل *Tefl*

Exercise 1: Match each word in (**A**) with its appropriate meaning in (**B**). **Remember to say the words out loud.**

B	A
but	مُرْهَق *murhaq*
now	يَبْدو *yabduu*
I work	أعْمَل *'aAmal*
it seems	الآن *al'aan*
God bless you!	قليلاً *qaliilan*
lecture	تَرْجَمَة *tarjama*
exhausted	لَكِن *laken*
excuse me	بَعْد إذْنك *baAd iThnak*
translation	مُحاضَرَة *muHaaDara*
little	سـلامَتك *Salaamatk*
possible to	يُمْكِن أن *yumken 'an*

91

Exercise 2: What does it mean?

Translation	Transliteration	Arabic
....	tab-baakh	طَبّاخ
....	rajul 'aAmaal	رَجُل أعمال
....	shurTy	شُرطي
....	Tabiib	طَبيب
....	muhandes	مُهَندس
....	muSaw-wer	مُصَوّر
....	muTreb	مُطْرِب
....	musiiqaar	موسـيقار
....	ras-saam	رَسّام
....	laaAeb	لاعِب

Exercise 3: Fill in the blanks using the vocabulary you have learned to make a dialogue.

M: What do you do?	M:	م: ....؟
A: I'm working at a translation office.	A:	أ: ....
M: That's good!	M:	م: ....
A: Yes. Excuse me. I have a lecture now.	A:	أ: ....
M: Okay, good-bye.	M: tafaD-Dal.	م: تَفَضّل؛ ....

Exercise 4: Translate into Arabic

1. How are you today?

....

2. You look exhausted!

....

3. Where is the translation office please?

....

4. Excuse me/ pardon, I have work now.

....

5. Actually I have a lecture today.

....

6. Actually I work in the daytime, and I study in the evening.

....

7. What do you do?

....

8- When do you work in the daytime?

....

9- When is the lecture?

....

10- Why do you work in the evening?

....

11- Why don't you work in the daytime?

....

12- What do you do in the evening?

....

Exercise 5: Write down the job of each picture

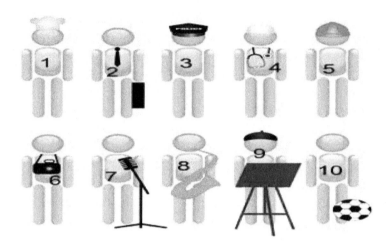

N	Transliteration	Arabic	N
1	....	....	1
2	....	....	2
3	....	....	3
4	....	....	4
5	....	....	5
6	....	....	6
7	....	....	7
8	....	....	8
9	....	....	9
10	....	....	10

Exercise 6: Use the prepositions and pronouns given in the brackets to express relationships of possession, association and accompaniment among humans and / or objects:

Transliteration	Arabic
1-john........ebn wa bint (L+huwa)	1- جون......... اِبْن وَ بِنْت.(لـ+هو)
2-.........'akh fii meSr (L+naHnu)	2-...........أخْ في مِصر.(لـ+نحن)
3-yaa maryam! hal.... dollar? (maAa+'anti)	3- يا مَرْيَم!هل.......دولار؟ (مَعَ+انتِ)
4-suzan .... Sadiiqa. (l+heya)	4- سـوزان ...... صَديقَة. (لـ+هي)
5-.....muHaaDra Tawiila al-yawm! (Aend+hum)	5-.......مُحاضَرَة طَويلَة اليوم! (عِند+هم)
6-hal......ketaab Arabii? (Aend+'antum)	6- هل.......كِتاب عَرَبي؟ (عِند+أنتم)
7-'akhy.......fii nfs alkuliya. (maAa+hum)	7- أَخي ......في نفس الكلية. (مع+هم)
8-hal......... say-yara? (maAa+'anta)	8- هَل ..... سَيّارة؟ (مَعَ+أنتَ)
9-......dirham emaraati.(maAa+anaa)	9-...... درهم إماراتي. (مَعَ+أنا)
10-aHmed.....Sadiiq fii nafs al-jaamiAa. (l+hwa)	10-أحمد........صديق في نفس الجامعة. (لـ+هو)

Exercise 7: Translate into Arabic

1-I don't have Emirati money.

....

2-We don't have a car.

....

3- Sarah doesn't have a lecture in the morning.

....

4- They don't have an Arabic book.

....

5- Don't you have work today?

....

Exercise 8: Give the plural for the befeminine words below

Transliteration	English	Arabic
saAa...........	hour	ساعَة...........
SafHa.........	page	صَفْحَة...........
waraqa.............	paper	ورَقَة...........
resaala..........	message	رِسالَة...........
jad-da.........	grandmother	جَدّة...........
Aam-ma........	aunt (paternal)	عَمّة...........
khala..........	aunt (maternal)	خالَة...........
benaaya......	building	بناية...........
Taawela.......	table	طاولة..........
Aada......	habit	عادَة...........

Exercise 9: <u>Guess</u> and underline the correct plural for the nouns below, note that with some of the plurals you see them for the first time, so you need to figure out the right ones to learn as you already know the difference between the feminine and the masculine nouns. The first one is already answered.

1- jadd........ (<u>'ajdaad</u>/jad-daat)   1- جَدّ .... (جَدات / <u>أجداد</u>)

2-Aamm........('aAmaam/Aam-maat)   2- عَمّ........... (أعْمام / عَمّات)

3- khaal........(khaalaat/ 'akhwaal)   3- خال .... (خالات / أخْوال)

4-'ab.........('abaa' / 'abaat)   4- أبّ .... (آباء / أبات)

5- umm........ ('amuun/ um-mhaat)   5- أمّ............. (أمون / أمهات)

6-kursy........(kursyaat/karaasy)   6- كرسي .... (كرسيات / كراسي)

7-ketaab.........(ketaabaat/kutub)   7- كتاب .... (كتابات / كُتُب)

8-Taaleb..........(Tul-laab/Taalebaat)   8- طالب .... (طُلّاب / طالِبات)

9- Taaleba........(Taalebaat/Tul-laab)   9- طالِبة .... (طالِبات / طُلّاب)

10- khaala........(khaalaat/ 'akhwaal)   10- خالَة .... (خالات / أخْوال)

Exercise 10: Complete the Arabic crossword puzzle! Write down the Arabic meaning

Across		Down
1- I work	2- Pardon	1- I study
3- He has		2- I have

Vocabulary

مُرْهَق
murhaq,exhausted

تَعبان
taAbaan,tired

يَبْدو
yabduu,it seems/ it looks like

أعْمَل
'aAmal,I work (verb)

العَمَل
alAamal,work (noun)

الشُّغْل
ash-shughl,work (noun)

الآن
al'aan,now

قليلًا
qaliilan,little

في
fii,in / at

تَرْجَمَة
tarjama,translation

لَكِن
laken,but

عَفْوَاً
Aafwan,pardon / excuse me

إِذْن
iThn,permission

بَعْد إِذْنك
baAd iThnek,excuse me

مُحاضَرَة
muHaaDara,lecture / presentaion

سلامَتك
salaamatk,God bless you! / get better

يُمْكِن أن
yumken 'an,possible to (polite request)

في الحقيقَة
fil Haqiiqa,actually / in fact / in reality

حقيقَة
Haqeeqa,reality

مُوَظَّف
muwaTH-THaf,employee

عِندي
Aendy,I have

بِسَبَب
be-sabab,because of

رَجُل أعمال
rajul 'aAmaal,business man

مُهَندس
muhandes,Engineer

شُرطي
shurTy,policeman

طَبيب
Tabiib,doctor

مُصَوِّر
muSaw-wer,photographer

طَبّاخ
tab-baakh,a cook

مُطْرِب
muTreb,singer

موسيقار
musiiqaar,musician

رَسّام
ras-saam,artist

لاعِب
laaAeb,player

UNIT SIX

In the Restaurant

UNIT SIX

In the Restaurant

Contents

- Dialogue

- Vocabulary

- Language notes

- Grammar usage

- Verbs

- Exercises

In the Restaurant

Fii l-maTAam في الْمَطْعَم

English	Transliteration	Arabic
Adam: Congratulation for your success at the exam Majed!	A: mabruuk en-najaaH fii elemteHaan ya majed!	آدَمْ: مَبْروك النَجَاح في الامْتِحان يا ماجِد.
Majed: God bless you, thanks Adam.	M: allah yubaarek fiik. shukran ya 'adam.	ماجِد: الله يُبارك فيك؛ شُكْراً يا آدَمْ.
Adam: I'm hungry. Would you like to go for lunch now?	A: 'anaa jawAaan. hal tuHeb 'an naTh-hab lelghadaa' al'an?	آدَم: أنا جَوْعان؛ هَلْ تُحِب أن نَذْهَب لِلغَداء الآن؟
Majed: Yes; I'm very hungry too.	M: naAam. wa 'anaa 'ayDan jawAaan jed-dan.	ماجِد: نَعَم؛ وَأنا أيْضاً جَوعان جِداً.

In the restaurant

Adam: May I have the menu please?	A: mumken elqaa'ema law samaHte?	آدَم: مُمْكِن القائِمة لَوْ سَمَحْتِ؟
Waitress: Here you are.	N: tafaD-Daluu.	النَادِلة: تَفَضّلوا.

Looking at the menu

Adam: What would you like to order Majed?	A: maThaa tuHeb 'an taTlub ya majed?	آدَم: مَاذا تُحِب أن تَطلُب يا ماجِد؟
Majed: I'll take salad, rice and chicken.	M: 'akhuTh salaTa wa urz wa dajaaj.	ماجِد: أخُذ سَلَطَة وَأرز وَدَجاج.
Adam: Me too. What would you like to drink?	A: wa 'anaa 'ayDan. wa maaThaa tashrab?	آدَم: وَأنا أيْضاً؛ وَماذا تَشْرَب؟
Majed: I'll drink orange juice. What would you like to drink?	M: 'ashrab AaSiir burtuqaal. wa 'anta, maaThaa tashrab?	ماجِد: أشْرَب عَصير بُرْتُقال. وَأنت؛ ماذا تَشرَب؟
Adam: Coffee with milk please. Without sugar, but after food.	A: mumken qahwa beHaliib. beduun suk-kar. wa laken baAd al'akl.	آدَم: مُمْكِن قَهْوَة بِحَليب. بِدُون سُكّر؛ وَلَكِن بَعْد الأكْل.

Vocabulary followed by unhighlighted sentences as an example

English	Transliteration	Arabic
restaurant	maTAam	مَطْعَم
'ayn al-maTAam al-Aaraby men faDlek?		أين المَطعم العربي من فضلك؟
congratulations	mabruuk	مَبْروك
mabruuk as-say-yaara aljadiida		مبروك السيارة الجديدة
God bless you	Allah yubaarek fiik	الله يُبارِك فيك
success	najaaH	نَجَاح
an-najaaH fil-Aamal SaAb		النجاح في العمل صعب
hungry	jawAaan/a	جَوْعان/ ـة
'anaa jawAaan jed-dan		أنا جوعان جِدّاً
exam	emteHaan	امْتِحان
Aendii emteHaan fil-Aaraby-ya al-yawm		عندي امتحان في العربية اليوم
I eat	'aa'kul	آكُل
breakfast	fuTuur / ifTaar	فُطور / إفطار
usually	Aadatan	عادةً
'aa'kul al-fuTuur Aadatan fil-maktab		أكل الفطور عادةً في المكتب
lunch	ghadaa'	غَداء
dinner	Aashaa'	عَشاء

	'aa'kul alghadaa' wal-Aashaa' fil-bayt	آكل الغداء والعشاء في البيت
menu	qaa'ema	قائِمة
possible (for polite requests)	mumken	مُمْكِن
	mumken el-qaa'ema men faDlek?	مُمكِن القائمة من فضلك؟
waiter	naadel/a	نَادِل/ ـة
	Sadiiqatii taAmal naadela	صديقتي تعمل نادِلة
I drink	'ashrab	أَشْرب
coffee	qahwa	قهوة
tea	shaay	شاي
	'ashrab qahwa fiS-SabaaH, wa shaay fil-masaa'	أشرَب قهوة في الصباح؛ وشاي بالنهار
orange	burtuqaal	بُرْتُقال
juice	ASiir	عصير
	mumken ASiir burtuqaal men faDlek!	مُمكِن عصير بُرتُقال من فضلك!
without	beduun	بِدُون
milk	laban Haliib	لَبَن حليب
sugar	suk-kar	سُكر
or	'aw	أو
	laa 'ashrab qahwa beduun Haliib 'aw suk-kar	لا أشرب قهوة بدون حليب أو سُكر
I want	uriid	أريد

rice	*urz*	أُرْز
salad	*salaTa*	سَلَطة
chicken	*dajaaj*	دَجَاج
uriid salaTa, wa urz wa dajaaj men faDlek		أريد سَلَطة؛ وأرز ودجاج من فضلك!
I like	*uHeb*	أحب
meat	*laHm*	لَحْم
fish	*samak*	سَمَك
uHeb as-samak, wa laa uHeb al-laHm		أحب السمك؛ ولا أحب اللحم
after	*baAd*	بَعْد
'ashrab shaay baAd al-ghadaa'		أشرب شاي بعد الغداء
but	*laken*	لَكِن
before	*qabl*	قَبْل
laa 'ashrab qahwa qabl al'akl		لا أشرب قهوة قبل الأكل
the bill	*faatuura*	فاتورَة
I pay	*'adfaA*	أَدْفَعْ
mumken 'adfaA el-faatuura men faDlek!		مُمكِن أدفع الفاتورة من فضلك!
bottle	*zujaaja*	زُجاجة
water	*maa' / meyaah*	ماء / مِياه
cold	*baared*	بارِد

hot	saakhen	ساخِن
uriid zujaaaja meyaah law samaHt		أريد زجاجة مياه لو سمحت
fried	maqly/a	مقلي / ـة
grilled	mashwy/a	مشوي / ـة
uHeb as-samak mashwy		أحب السمك مشوي
spicy	Haar	حارْ
salt	melH	مِلْح
pepper	felfel	فِلفِل
ice	thalj	ثَلْج

Say it in Arabic

1- Where is the Arabic restaurant please?

2- Congratulations for the new house

3- Success is beautiful but hard

4- I'm so hungry

5- I have a test at work

6- I don't eat breakfast at home, I eat lunch at work

7- I drink orange juice before dinner

8- I drink coffee without milk and sugar after lunch

9- May i have rice, salad and chicken please?

10- I don't eat meat, but I eat fish

11- I usually pay the bill before I eat

12- I don't drink cold water

Fill in the blanks with one of the new words

1- Sadiiqatii naadela fii .... Araby

1- صديقتي نادلة في .... عربي.

2- .... as-say-yaara aljadiida yaa aHmad

2- .... السيارة الجديدة يا أحمد.

3- 'anaa .... jed-dan, uriid an 'aa'kul

3- أنا .... جدا! أريد أن آكل.

4- laa .... qahwa fil-masaa'

4- لا .... قهوة في المساء.

5- 'ashrab .... ASiir burtoqaal

Aadatan qabl al-ghadaa'

5- أشرب .... برتقال عادة قبل الغداء.

6- men faDlek, uriid .... beduun

.... 'aw suk-kar

6- من فضلك؛ أريد .... بدون

.... أو سكر.

7- laa 'aa'kul laHm 'aw .... Aadatan fil-

Ashaa', wa laken 'aa'kul samak

7- لا آكل لحم أو .... عادة في العشاء؛ ولكن آكل سمك.

8- mumken .... meyaah baareda!

8- ممكن .... مياه باردة!

Look at the picture and learn these words

N	Transliteration	Arabic	N
1	*dajaaj*	دَجاج	1
2	*shuurba*	شوربة	2
3	*laHm*	لَحْم	3
4	*salaTa*	سَلَطة	4
5	*samak*	سَمَك	5
6	*naqaaneq*	نَقانِق	6

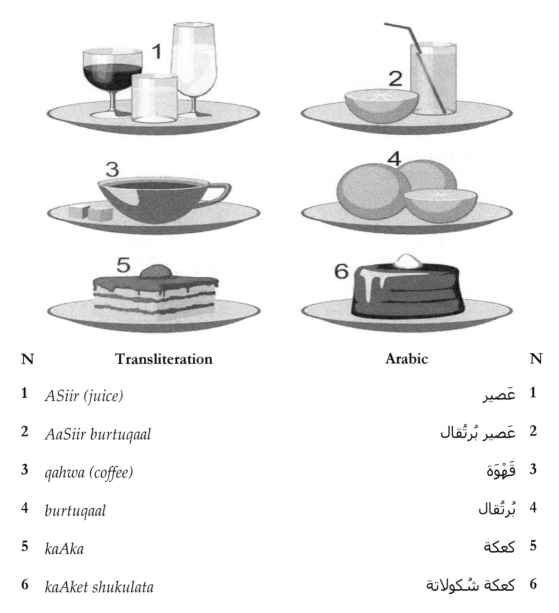

N	Transliteration	Arabic	N
1	*ASiir (juice)*	عَصير	1
2	*AaSiir burtuqaal*	عَصير بُرتُقال	2
3	*qahwa (coffee)*	قَهْوَة	3
4	*burtuqaal*	بُرتُقال	4
5	*kaAka*	كعكة	5
6	*kaAket shukulata*	كعكة شُكولاتة	6

Language Notes

Most Arabic speakers use an expression to say "me also/as well" in their dialects not as in standard Arabic, they say in most of the Arabic dialects "*wa 'anaa kamaa 'an*", as "*kamaa 'an*" "كَما أَن" means as well.

Grammar usage

az-zaman elHaaDer الزّمَن الحاضِر

The Present Tense

You have seen Adam in the dialogue says (*'a'kul* = I eat – *'ashrab* = I drink – *'adrus* = I study). These words are Arabic verbs in present tense. If you had said "I eat", it would be equal to saying "I am eating" in Arabic. Also *'ashrab* means "I drink" or "I am drinking", because Arabic has just one present tense.

In Arabic, the verb itself has the subject. As its expressed in a prefix = letter at the beginning / or a prefix and a suffix = letter at the end and the beginning of the verb.

This means that all verbs in the Arabic language are regular! You don't need to change the root of the verb for any tense neither past nor present or future. So, to express "I eat" or "I'm eating" you don't need to say *"'anaa 'a'kul"*, you can simply say *"'a'kul"* without a pronoun, as the verb itself tells about the speaker.

The table below lists the full conjugation of the present tense of the verb "**to live**".

English	Transliteration	Arabic	Pro	
I live	*'askun*	أسْكُن	أنا *'anaa*	First person
We live	*naskun*	نَسْكُن	نَحْن *naHnu*	
You live (male)	*taskun*	تَسْكُن	أنْتَ *'anta*	Second person
You live (female)	*taskunii / taskuniin*	تَسْكُنـي /تَسْكُنـين	أنْتِ *'anti*	
You live (plural)	*taskunuu /taskunuun*	تَسْكُنـوا /تَسْكُنـون	أنتم *'antum*	
He lives	*yaskun*	يَسْكُن	هُوَ *huwa*	Third person
She lives	*taskun*	تَسْكُن	هِيَ *heya*	
They live	*yaskunuu /yaskunuun*	يَسْكُنـوا / يَسْكُنـون	هُمْ *hum*	

As you can see in the table, there are two forms for the verb with the pronouns (you for a female, you for plural and they). A form with the ending "*uu*" and the other one with "*uun*", both of them have a grammatical usage in formal Arabic, which you will learn about in the intermediate level. While most Arabic speakers use the ones with "*uu*" at the end, many Gulf Arabs use the form with the ending "*uun*".

To eat

English	Transliteration	Arabic	Pro
I eat	'a'kul	آكُلْ	أنا 'anaa
We eat	na'kul	نَأكُل	نَحْنُ naHnu
You eat (male)	ta'kul	تَأكُل	أنْتَ 'anta
You eat (female)	ta'kulii / ta'kuliin	تَأكُلي / تَأكُلين	أنْتِ 'anti
You eat (plural)	ta'kuluu /ta'kuluun	تَأكلـوا / تَأكُلون	أنتم 'antum
He eats	ya'kul	يَأكُل	هُوَ huwa
She eats	ta'kul	تَأكُل	هِيَ heya
They eat	ya'kuluu /ya'kuluun	يَأكُلـوا /يَأكُلون	هُمْ hum

To drink

English	Transliteration	Arabic	Pro
I drink	'ashrab	أشْرَب	أنا 'anaa
We drink	nashrab	نَشرَب	نَحْنُ naHnu
You drink (male)	tashrab	تَشرَب	أنْتَ 'anta
You drink (female)	tashrabii /tashrabiin	تَشْرَبي / تَشْرَبين	أنْتِ 'anti
You drink (plural)	tashrabuu /tashrabuun	تَشرَبـوا / تَشْرَبون	أنتم 'antum
He drinks	yashrab	يَشْرَب	هُوَ huwa
She drinks	tashrab	تَشرَب	هِيَ heya
They drink	yashrabuu /yashrabuun	يشْرَبـوا /يَشْرَبـون	هُمْ hum

To take

English	Transliteration	Arabic	Pro
I take	'a'khuTh	آخُذ	أنا 'anaa
We take	na'khuTh	نَأخُذ	نَحْنُ naHnu
You take (male)	ta'khuTh	تَأخُذ	أنْتَ 'anta
You take (female)	ta'khuThii /ta'khuThiin	تَأخُذي /تَأخُذين	أنْتِ 'anti
You take (plural)	ta'khuThuu /ta'khuThuun	تَأخُذوا /تَأخُذون	أنتم 'antum
He takes	ya'khuTh	يَأخُذ	هُوَ huwa
She takes	ta'khuTh	تَأخُذ	هِيَ heya
They take	ya'khuThuu /ya'khuThuun	يَأخُذوا /يَأخُذون	هُمْ hum

To order

English	Transliteration	Arabic	Pro
I order	'aTlub	أطلُب	'anaa أنا
We order	naTlub	نَطلُب	naHnu نَحْن
You order (male)	taTlub	تَطلُب	'anta أنْتَ
You order (female)	taTlubii /taTlubiin	تَطلُبي /تَطلُبِين	'anti أنْتِ
You order (plural)	taTlubuu /taTlubuun	تَطلُبوا/ تَطلُبون	'antum أنتم
He orders	yaTlub	يطلُب	huwa هُوَ
She orders	taTlub	تَطلُب	heya هِيَ
They order	yaTlubuu /yaTlubuun	يَطلُبوا /يَطلُبون	hum هُمْ

To like

English	Transliteration	Arabic	Pro
I like	'auHebb	أحِبّ	'anaa أنا
We like	nuHebb	نُحِبّ	naHnu نَحْن
You like (male)	tuHebb	تُحِب	'anta أنْتَ
You like (female)	tuHebbii /tuHebbiin	تُحِبّي /تُحِبّين	'anti أنْتِ
You like (plural)	tuHebbuu / tuHebbuun	تُحِبّوا /تُحِبّون	'antum أنتم
He likes	yuHebb	يُحِبّ	huwa هُوَ
She likes	tuHebb	تُحِبّ	heya هِيَ
They like	yuHebbuu / yuHebbuun	يُحِبّوا /يُحِبّون	hum هُمْ

To want

English	Transliteration	Arabic	Pro
I want	'auriid	أريد	'anaa أنا
We want	nuriid	نُريد	naHnu نَحْن
You want (male)	turiid	تُريد	'anta أنْتَ
You want (female)	turiidii /turiidiin	تُريدي / تُريدين	'anti أنْتِ
You want (plural)	turiiduu /turiiduun	تُريدوا / تُريدون	'antum أنتم
He wants	yuriid	يُريد	huwa هُوَ
She wants	turiid	تُريد	heya هِيَ
They want	yuriiduu /yuriiduun	يُريدوا / يُريدون	hum هُمْ

To study

English	Transliteration	Arabic	Pro
I study	*'adrus*	أدْرُس	أنا *'anaa*
We study	*nadrus*	نَدْرُس	نَحْن *naHnu*
You study (male)	*tadrus*	تَدْرُس	أنْتَ *'anta*
You study (female)	*tadrusii /tadrusiin*	تَدْرُسـي / تَدْرُسـين	أنْتِ *'anti*
You study (plural)	*tadrusuu /tadrusuun*	تَدْرُسـوا / تَدْرُسـون	أنتم *'antum*
He studies	*yadrus*	يَدْرُس	هُوَ *huwa*
She studies	*tadrus*	تَدْرُس	هيَ *heya*
They study	*yadrusuu /yadrusuun*	يَدْرُسـوا /يَدْرُسـون	هُمْ *hum*

Negation of the Present

To negate the present tense we have learned, just use the particle "لا"-"*Laa*"before the verb. For example, to say (I don't eat, don't drink, I don't study).

Laa 'a'kul – laa 'ashrab – laa 'adrus   لا آكل – لا أشـرب - لا أدرس

Visit the book website to find out more!
http://www.LetsTalkArabic.com

Exercise 1 : Choose the correct answer

1- 'adam .... fii madiina saghiira.   1- آدم .... في مَدينة صَغَيَرة.

3- أسكُن 'askun	يَسكُن 2- yaskun	تَسكُن 1- taskun

2- laa .... Dajaaj Haar ya Muhammad   2- لا............. دجاج حارّ يا مُحَمَّد.

3- تَأكُل ta'akul	تَأكُلي 2- ta'akulii	يَأكُل 1- ya'akul

3-'akhii .... Fii jaameAat Princeton.   3- أخي .... في جامعة برينستون

3- يَدْرُس yadrus	أدْرُس 2- 'adrus	يَدْرُسـون 1- yadrusuun

4- men faDlek, 'anaa .... AaSiir burtuqaal.   4- مِن فَضلِك؛ انا .... عَصير بُرْتُقال .

3- يُريدوا turiiduu	تُريد 2- turiid	أريد 1- uriid

5- maaThaa .... 'an taTlub yaa kariim.?   5- ماذا .... أن تَطَلَّب يا كريم ؟

3- تَحبوا tuHebuu	تُحِب 2- tuHeb	يُـحِب 1- yuHeb

6- 'abii .... qahwa fii S-SabaaH.   6- أبي .... قَهْوَة في الصباح

3- تَشْرَب tashrab	يَشْرَب 2- yashrab	يَأكُل 1- ya'kul

7-...... maAa 'ausratii fii bayt kabiir.   7- .... مع أسرتي في بيت كبير.

3- أسكُن 'askun	يَسكُن 2- yaskun	تَسكُن 1- taskun

8- 'anaa jawAaan .... sanwich   8- أنا جوعان .... سَنْدويتش

3- يُريدوا turiiduu	تُريد 2- turiid	أريد 1- uriid

Exercise 2: Translate into Arabic

1- Where do you live?

……………………………………………………………………..

2-I live and work in Qatar.

……………………………………………………………………..

3- I like to drink coffee in the morning.

……………………………………………………………………..

4- Do you want to order now?

……………………………………………………………………..

5- Do you like Arabic food?

……………………………………………………………………..

6- She doesn`t like tea, she likes coffee.

……………………………………………………………………..

7- In this restaurant, we eat beautiful Arabic food.

……………………………………………………………………..

8- I like Arabic language.

……………………………………………………………………..

9-The students don`t want to study hard (well = *jay-yedan* جيداً).

……………………………………………………………………..

10- We don`t want to eat now.

……………………………………………………………………..

11- I like Turkish coffee

……………………………………………………………………..

12- I'm hungry

……………………………………………………………………..

Exercise 3: Conjugate these verbs

English	Transliteration	Arabic
I write	'aktub	أكتُب
I know	'aAref	أعْرِف
I understand	'afham	أفْهِم
I hear	'asmaA	أسْمَع
I read	'aqra'	أقْرأ
I sit	'ajles	أجْلِس
I go out	'akhruj	أخْرُج
I listen	'astameA	أسْتَمِع
I wake up	'aS-Huu	أصْحو
I sleep	'anaam	أنَام
I watch	'aushaahed	أشاهِد
I travel	'ausaafer	أسافِر
I go	'aTh-hab	أذهَب
I come	'ajii'	أجيء
I speak	'atakal-lam	أتَكَلّم
I say	'aquul	أقول
I see	'ashuuf	أشـوف

English	Transliteration	Arabic	Pro
'anaa			أنا
naHnu			نَحْن
'anta			أنْت
'ante			أنْتِ
'antum			أنتم
huwa			هُوَ
heya			هِيَ
hum			هُمْ

English	Transliteration	Arabic	Pro
'anaa			أنا
naHnu			نَحْن
'anta			أنْت
'ante			أنْتِ
'antum			أنتم
huwa			هُوَ
heya			هِيَ
hum			هُمْ

Exercise 4: Match the picture with the meaning.

دَجاج *dajaaj*

شـوربة *shuurb*

لَحْم *laHm*

قَهْوَة *qahwa*

سَلَطة *salaTa*

سَمَك *samak*

Exercise 5: What is this? Write down the meaning of what is in the picture.

N	Transliteration	Arabic	N
1	....	....	1
2	....	....	2
3	....	....	3
4	....	....	4
5	....	....	5
6	....	....	6

Exercise 6: Build the dialogue.

Adam: What would you like to order Majed?	A:.............................. ....?	.... :آدَم ؟.....................
Majed: I'll take salad, rice and chicken.	M:..............................	.... :ماجِد ....
Adam: Me too. What would you like to drink?	A:.............................. ....?	.... :آدَم ؟.....................
Majed: I'll drink orange juice. You, what would you like to drink?	M:.............................. ....?	.... :ماجِد ؟ ....
Adam: Coffee with milk please. Without sugar; but after eating.	A..............................	.... :آدَم ....

Exercise 7: Can you find 4 words you have learned in the word square? Write out the meanings of the words you have found as in the example.

1- *Chicken*.....................

2- ....

3- ....

4- ....

5- ....

ظ	غ	ع	ج	ا	ج	د
ء	ح	ل	م	ت	ي	ب
ا	ب	ح	د	ر	ا	ب
ة	س	ر	ا	ح	ﻫ	ا
ة	ط	ل	س	ص	ج	د

Exercise 8: What does it mean?

English	Transliteration	Arabic
....	maTAam	مَطْعَم
....	mabruuk	مَبْروك
....	jawAaan	جَوْعان
....	emteHaan	امْتِحان
....	fuTuur / ifTaar	فُطور / إفطار
....	ghadaa'	غَداء
....	Aashaa'	عَشاء
....	qaa'ma	قائِمة
....	beduun	بِدُون
....	'adfaA	أدْفَعْ
....	el-faatuura	الفاتورَة
....	zujaaja	زُجاجة
....	maa' / meyaah	ماء / مِياه
....	melH	مِلْح
....	Haar	حارْ
....	baared	بارِد
....	saakhen	ساخِن
....	thalj	ثَلْج

Exercise 9: How do you say in Arabic?

English	Transliteration	Arabic
I work	....	....
I know	....	....
I understand	....	....
I hear	....	....
I read	....	....
I sit	....	....
I go out	....	....
I listen	....	....
I speak	....	....
I write	....	....
I watch	....	....
I travel	....	....

Exercise 10: Complete the Arabic crossword puzzle! Write down the Arabic meaning of the verbs.

Down

1- I drink

2- I hear

Cross

1- I order   3- I work

2- I know

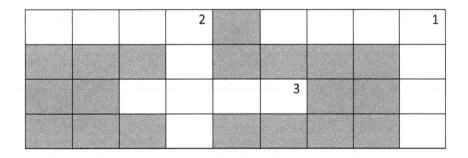

121

Exercise 11: What they are doing? make a sentence in Arabic about each picture

Vocabulary

مَطْعَم
maTAam,restaurant

مَبْروك
mabruuk,congratulations

نَجَاح
najaaH,success

الله يُبارِك فيك
Allah yubaarek fiik,God bless you
(response for mabruuk)

جَوْعان
jawAaan,hungry

اِمْتِحان
emteHaan,exam / test

آكُل
'aa'kul,I eat

فُطور / اِفطار
fuTuur / ifTaar,breakfast

غَداء
ghadaa',lunch

عَشاء
Aashaa',dinner

قائِمة
qaa'ma,menu

نَادِل
naadel,waiter

أَشرب
'ashrab,I drink

خُبز
khubz,bread

عصير
ASiir,juice

بِدُون
beduun,without

لَبَن حليب
laban Haliib,milk

عادَة
Aaadatan,usually

أريد
uriid,I want

قهوة
qahwa,coffee

سُكر
suk-kar,sugar

أُرز
urz,rice

سَلَطة
salaTa,salad

دَجَاج
dajaaj,chicken

لَحْم
laHm,meat

سَمَك
samak,fish

بَعْد
baAd,after

قَبْل
qabl,before

لَكِن
laken,but

أَدْفَع
'adfaA,I pay

الفاتورَة
el-faatuura,the bill

زُجاجة
zujaaja,bottle

ماء / مياه
maa' / meyaah,water

مِلْح
melH,salt

فلفِل
felfel,pepper

حَارّ
Haar,spicy

بارِد
baared,cold

ساخِن
saakhen,hot

ثَلْج
thalj,ice

شوربة
shuurba,soup

أَسْكُن

123

أطْلُب
'aTlub,I order

أحِبّ
oHebb,I like / I love

أكْتُب
'aktub,I write

أعرِف
'aAref,I know

أفْهم
'afham,I understand

أسْمَع
'asmaA,I hear

أقْرأ
'aqra',I read

أجْلِس
'ajles,I sit

أخْرُج
'akhruj,I go out

أسْتَمِع
'astameA,I listen

أصْحو
'aS-Huu,I wake up

أنَام
'anaam,I sleep

أشاهِد
'aushaahed,I watch

أسافر
'ausaafer,I travel

أذهَب
'aTh-hab,I go

أجيء
'ajii',I come

أتَكَلّم
'atakal-lam,I speak

أقول
'aquul,I say

أشوف
'ashuuf,I see

'askun,I live

آخُذ
'akhuTh,I take

مقلي / ـة
maqly/a,fried

مشوي / ـة
mashwy/a,grilled

UNIT SEVEN
Asking for Directions

UNIT SEVEN

Asking for Directions

Contents

- Dialogue

- Vocabulary

- Numbers and the time

- Grammar usage

- Exercises

Asking for Directions
Alet-tejaahaat الاتِّجاهات

English	Transliteration	Arabic
Majed: Excuse me, do you know where is the post office please?	M: law samHat hal taAref 'ayna maktab albariid men faDlek?	ماجِد: لَو سَمَحْت: هَلْ تَعْرِف أَيْن مَكْتَب البَريد مِن فَضلِك؟
Traffic Officer: Sure, it's close to here, you can walk straight until you get to the end of the street.	O: 'akiid; fahuwa qariib men hunaa , yumkenuka 'an tamshii Aalaa Tuul le'akher ash-shariiA.	ضَابِط المُرور: أكيد؛ فَهُوَ قَريب مِن هُنا، يُمْكِنك أَنْ تَمْشي عَلَى طُول لِآخِر الشَّارِع.
Majed: How far it is almost?	M: wa, kam elmsaafa taqriiban?	ماجِد: وَكَمْ المَسافَة تَقْريباً؟
The officer: About 6 buildings, at first traffic light turn right, so the post office is there.	O: baAd Hawaalii set benaayaat, Aend 'aw-wal esharat muruur, talef ela alyamiin, famaktab el-bariid hunaak.	الضَّابِط: بَعْدِ حَوالَي سِت بِنايات؛ عِنْد أَوَّل إشارَة مُرور؛ تَلَف إلَى اليَمين؛ فَمَكْتب البَريد هُناك.
Majed: On which side of the road?	M: Aalaa ayy jaaneb men aT-Tariiq?	ماجِد: عَلَى أي جَانِب مَن الطَّريق؟
The officer: On the left side, before the Lebanese restaurant.	O: Aalaa a-sh-shemaal, qabl almaTAam al-lebnaanii.	الضَّابِط: عَلَى الشِّمال؛ قَبْل المَطْعَم اللُّبْنانيّ.
Majed : Thanks a lot mister officer.	M:Shukran kaTheran HaDret eD-DaabeT.	ماجِد: شُكْراً كَثيراً حَضْرة الضَّابِط.
The officer: Not at all, good-bye.	O: Afwan. maA alsalaama.	الضَّابِط: عَفْواً؛ مَعَ السَّلامَة.

Vocabulary

English	Transliteration	Arabic
front of	'amaam	أمام
'askun 'amaam al-JaameA'a		أسكن أمام الجامعة
behind	waraa'	وَراء
say-yaratii waraa' al-bayt		سيارتي وراء البيت
officer	Daabet	ضابِط
police	shurTa	شُرطة
Sadiiqii Daabet shurTa		صديقي ضابط شُرطة
straight away /ahead	Aalaa Tuul	عَلَى طُول
I go	'aTh-hab	أذهب
'aTh-hab ilal-bayt Aalaa Tuul baAd alAamal		أذهب إلى البيت على طول بعد العمل
beside	be-jaaneb	بِجَانِب
baytii be-jaaneb almadrasa		بيتي بجانب المدرسة
directions	et-tejaahaat	اتّجاهات
street	shariiA	شارِع
laa 'aAref et-tejaahaat haThaa ash-shaareA		لا أعرف اِتّجاهات هذا الشارع
road	Tariiq	طَريق
haThaa Tariiq Tawiil jed-dan		هذا طريق طويل جِدّاً
station	maHaT-Ta	مَحَطّة

petrol station	maHaT-Tat banziin	مَحَطّة بَنْزين
	'ayn maHaT-Tat al-metruu men faDlek?	أين محطة المترو من فضلك؟
building	benaaya	بِنايَة
	maktabii fii haThehel benaaya	مكتبي في هَذِهِ البناية
hotel	funduq	فُنْدُق
museum	matHaf	مَتْحَف
square	maydaan	مَيدان
	al-funduq waraa' al-matHaf al-meSryy	الفُندق وراء المتحف المصري
post office	maktab el-bariid	مَكْتَب البَريد
right	yamiin	يَمين
left	shemaal / yasaar	شِمال / يَسار
	hunaak maktab bariid Aala al-yamiin	هناك مكتب بريد على اليمين
traffic light	eshaarat muruur	إشارة مُرور
	hunaak eshaarat muruur fii haThaa ash-shaareA	هناك إشارة مرور في هذا الشارع
distance	masaafa	مَسافَة
	al-masaafa men al-maktab ilaa baytii qariiba	المسافة من بيتي إلى المكتب قريبة
airport	maTaar	مَطار
	taxi; uriid 'an 'aTh-hab ilaal-maTaar	تاكسي: أريد أن أذهب إلى المطار
you (formal)	HaDret	حَضْرَة
	HaDretak meSryy? laa suuryy	حضرتك مصري؟ لا سوري

Say it in Arabic

1- My car is in front of your car

2- My house is behind the French restaurant

3- My friend is a police officer

4- Can we go straight?

5- I'm sitting beside Sara

6- Do you know the directions?

7- Do you live on this street?

8- My work is from this way

9- Is there a petrol station nearby?

10- What is this building called?

11- Is this a good hotel?

12- The museum is so close!

13- Is there a post office here please?

14- My car is on the right side of this building

15- How can I go to the airport please?

16- Where is the metro station please?

Fill in blanks with one of the new words

1- 'ayn 'anta? 'anaa hunaa .... al-bayt.

١- أين أنت؟ أنا هنا .... البيت.

2- say-yaaratii .... haThehe elbenaaya

٢- سيارتي .... هذه البناية.

3- Sadiiqii yaAmal .... shuTa.

٣- صديقي يعمل .... شرطة.

4- hal taAref .... ilaa shaareA' al-et-teHaad.

٤- هل تعرف .... إلى شارع الاتحاد؟

5- law samaHt, hal hunaak .... banziin qariiba men hunaa?

٥- لو سمحت؛ هل هناك .... بنزين قريبة من هنا؟

6- 'askun bejaaneb .... hilton

٦- أسكن بجانب .... هيلتون.

7- al-funduq 'amaam .... al-maSryy fii maydaan at-taHriir.

٧- الفندق أمام .... المصري في ميدان التحرير.

Learn these words

English	Transliteration	Arabic
hour/ watch	*saaAa*	ساعة
laa 'akhruj men al-bayt qabl as-saAa 10 SabaHan		لا أخرج من البيت قبل الساعة 10 ص
day	*yawm*	يوم
laa 'aTh-hab lelAamal yawm aljumuAa		لا أذهب للعمل يوم الجُمعة
week / weeks	*'asbuuA / 'asaabeeA*	أُسْبُوع / أسابيع
'anaa mashghuul jed-dan haThaa al-'asbuuA		أنا مشغول جدا هذا الأسبوع
month / months	*shahr / shuhuur*	شَـهْر / شُـهور
yabduu haTha ash-shahr Tawiil jed-dan		يبدو هذا الشهر طويل جدا
year / years	*sana / seniin*	سَنَة/ سنين
uriid an usaafer lesana baAd al-jaameAa		أريد أن أسافر لسنة بعد الجامعة

century / centuries	qarn / quruun	قَرْن/ قُرون
time	waqt	وَقْت
don't / not	laysa	ليس
laysa Aendii waqt al-yawm		ليس عندي وقت اليوم
quarter	rubA	رُبْع
third	thulth	ثُلْث
'ashuufak baAd rubA 'aw thulth saAa		أشوفك بعد ربع أو ثلث ساعة
Less: literally: except	il-la	إلّا_
'akhruj men almaktab as-SaAa 5 il-la rubA		أخرج من المكتب الساعة 5 إلا رُبع
second	thaanya	ثانية
thaanya waaHeda men faDlek!		ثانية واحدة من فضلك!
minute / minutes	daqeeqa / daqaa'eq	دَقيقَة / دَقائِق
usually	Aadatan	عادةً
uriid 5 'aw 10 daqaa'eq leS-Salaa Aadatan		أريد 5 أو 10 دقائق للصلاة عادةً
sometimes	'aHyaanan	أحياناً
uHeb alAamal fil-masaa' 'aHyaanan		أحب العمل في المساء أحيانا
always	daa'eman	دائما
'aTh-hab ilal-Aamal daa'eman qabl as-saAa 8		أذهب إلى العمل دائما قبل الساعة 8
rarely	naaderan	نادراً
ushaahed at-televziuun naaderan		أشاهد التلفزيون نادراً

immediately	*Haalan*	حالاً
uriid 'an 'aThhab Haalan		أريد أن أذهب حالاً
after	*baAd*	بَعْد
'ashrab qahwa baAd al-fuTuur		أشرب قهوة بعد الفطور
before	*qabl*	قَبْل
laa 'anaam qabl as-saAa 10 masaa'an		لا أنام قبل الساعة 10 مساء

Say it in Arabic

1- It takes one hour to go to work

2- We have a long day at work

3- I'm so busy this week

4- I'm traveling this month

5- I want to study Arabic for a year

6- I want to speak to you for 5 minutes

7- I usually don't go out on Friday

8- Sometimes I work in the evening, but I like to waork always in the morning

9- I want to go immediately

10- See you after work

LOOK AT THE PICTURE AND LEARN THESE WORDS:

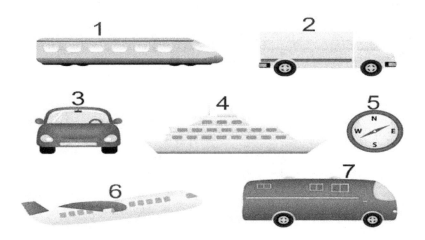

Transliteration		Arabic
N		**N**
1	qeTaar	قِطار 1
2	shaaHena	شاحِنة 2
3	say-yaara	سَيّارة 3
4	safiina	سَفينة 4
5	buuSla	بوصلة 5
6	Taa'era	طائِرة 6
7	Haafela	حافِلَة 7

The table below shows the Arabic numbers from Zero to Ten

The numerals used in English are of Arabic origin, but Arabs nowadays use the Hindi ones sometimes, because of business ties with India in the past.

Transliteration	Arabic script	Arabic Numeral
Sefr	صِفْر	0
waHed	واحِد	1
'ethnaan/'ethnayn	اثنان / إِثْنَين	2
thalatha	ثَلاثَة	3
'arbaAa	أَرْبَعَة	4
khamsa	خَمْسة	5
set-ta	سِتَّة	6
sabAa	سَبْعَة	7
thamaaneya	ثَمانِية	8
tesAa	تِسْعَة	9
Aashara	عَشَرَة	10

Days of the week are mostly driven from numbers as per the following table.

Days of the week

English	Transliteration	Arabic
Sunday	yawm el-'aHad	يَوْم الأَحَد
Monday	yawm el-ethnayn	يَوْم الإِثْنَين
Tuesday	yawm ethulathaa'	يَوْم الثُلاثاء
Wednesday	yawm el-arbeAa'	يَوْم الأَرْبعاء
Thursday	yawm el-khamees	يَوْم الخَميس
Friday	yawm el-jumuAa	يَوْم الجُمعَة
Saturday	yawm as-sabt	يَوْم السّبْت

Months

English	Transliteration	Arabic
January	*yanayer*	يناير
February	*fubrayer*	فبراير
March	*maares*	مارس
April	*'abriil*	ابريل
May	*mayuu*	مايو
June	*yuunyuu*	يونيو
July	*yuulyuu*	يوليو
August	*'aughusTus*	أغسطس
September	*sebtamber*	سبتمبر
October	*'auktober*	أكتوبر
November	*nuufamber*	نوفمبر
December	*diisamber*	ديسمبر

As you see the above table shows the Arabized months from the Latin ones. Also there are the Arabic months which are used for the Islamic calendar. Those months depend on the __lunar__ calendar.

muHar-ram, Safar, rabiiA 'aw-wal, rabiiA thaanii, jumaad 'aw-wal, jumaad thaanii, rajab, shaAbaan, ramadaan, shaw-waal, Thu l-qeAda,

Thu l-Hej-ja.

مُحَرّم، صَفَر، رَبِيع أوّل، رَبِيع ثاني، جُماد أولى، جُمادى ثانية، رَجَب، شَعْبان، رَمَضان، شَوّال، ذو القِعْدة، ذو الحِجّة.

Arabic ordinal numbers can be easily distinguished from the numbers used in counting. The table below includes the numbers first to twelfth, they are presented together with the definite article. This is the form used in telling the time.

Ordinal Numbers

The first	al-'aw-wal	الأوّل
The second	ath-thaanii	الثّاني
The third	ath-thaaleth	الثّالِث
The fourth	ar-raabeA	الرّابِع
The fifth	al-khaames	الخامِس
The sixth	as-saades	السّادِس
The seventh	as-saabeA	السّابِع
The eighth	ath-thaamen	الثّامِن
The ninth	at-taaseA	التّاسِع
The tenth	al-Aaasher	العاشِر
The eleventh	al-Hadii Aashar	الحادِي عَشَر
The twelfth	ath-thaanii Aashar	الثّاني عَشَر

Grammar usage

1-Please note that the number has got to have the same gender as the noun! As below:

English	Transliteration	Arabic
One book	*ketaab waaHed*	كتاب واحد
One message	*resaala waaHeda*	رِسالة واحدة
Two (m)students	*Taalebaan ethnaan*	طالبـان اثنـان
Two (f)students	*Taalebataan ethnataan*	طالبـتان اثنـتان

Arabic has a **dual form** which is used by adding ان-ين to the noun as in "*Taaleb/Taalebaan* or *Taalebain*" طالب- طالبان / طالبين so the meaning will be "two students". The same thing with the feminine nouns by adding (ان-ين) with just one more thing the *taa Marbuuta* at the end of the feminine noun ـة becomes *taa maftuuha* ت before adding the suffixes ان-ين las in "*Taaleba/Taalebataan* or *Taalebatain*" طالبة- طالبتان/ طالبتين to say "two female students".

2- When you count from 3 to 10, use the plural for the counted nouns. For example,

thalaath say-yaraat, Aashar say-yaaraat

ثلاث سيارات، عَشـر سيارات.

But after 10, use the singular nouns again, even for billions. For example:

Ahada Aashar say-yaara, melyuun say-yaara

أَحَّدَ عَشـر سيارة؛ مليون سيارة

What is the time?

كَمْ السَّاعَة؟

Kam es-saaAa?

The ordinal numbers are used in formal Arabic to tell the time. For example, if it is 1:15, you simply say in Arabic, "*al-waaHeda wa rubuA*"

And "*wa thuluth*" for 1:20, and "wa neSf" for 1:30, and "*ethnain 'el-laa thuluth*" for 1:40, and "*ethnain 'el-laa rubuA*" for 1:45.

Exercise 1: Can you find the 4 Arabic meanings for the words in the word square below?

1- Always

2- Sometimes

3- Rarely

4- Usually

5- Immediately

ي	د	ا	ئ	م	اَ	ر
اَ	ح	ي	ا	ن	اَ	ز
ك	ن	ا	د	ر	اَ	ى
ع	ا	د	ةَ	ي	ر	ف
ق	ح	ا	ل	اَ	ن	و

Exercise 2: Using the words below, fill in the puzzle with the meanings. Remember to go from right to left or up to down.

Down

1- a second

Across

2- hour

3- minute

4- week

5- month

Exercise 3: Translate into Arabic

1- Excuse me; do you know where the restaurant is please?

....

2- Sure, you can walk ahead until you get to the end of this street.

....

3- How far is it?

....

4- On which side of the road?

....

5- On the left side, before the post office.

....

6- Do you know the directions to the train station?

....

7- Where is the bus station please?

....

8- Where is the airport please?

....

9- Where is the petrol station please?

....

10- Where is the Egyptian museum please?

....

Exercise 4: Match the picture with the meaning.

قِطار qeTaar

سَيّارة say-yaara

شاحِنة shaaHena

حافِلَة Haafela

سَفينة safiina

بوصلة buuSla

Exercise 5: Conjugate the verbs below

English	Transliteration	Arabic	Pro
I go	'aTh-hab	أذهَب	أنا 'anaa
We go			نَحْن naHnu
You go (male)			أنْتَ 'anta
You go (female)			أنْتِ 'anti
You go (plural)			أنتم 'antum
He goes			هُوَ huwa
She goes			هِيَ heya
They go			هُمْ hum

English	Transliteration	Arabic	Pro
I walk	'amshii	أمْشي	أنا 'anaa
We walk			نَحْن naHnu
You walk (male)			أنْتَ 'anta
You walk (female)			أنْتِ 'anti
You walk (plural)			أنتم 'antum
He walks			هُوَ huwa
She walks			هِيَ heya
They walk			هُمْ hum

Exercise 6: Complete the numbers from zero to ten in Arabic.

Number	Transliteration	Arabic script
0	*Sefr*	صِفْر
1	*waHed*	واحِد
2	………………..	……………...
3	……………...	……………...
4	………………..	……………...
5	………………..	……………...
6	………………..	……………...
7	………………..	……………...
8	………………..	……………...
9	………………..	……………...
10	………………..	……………...

Exercise 7: Complete the days of the week in Arabic.

English	Transliteration	Arabic
Sunday	*yawm el-'aHad*	يَوْم الأَحَد
Monday	…………………..	………………….
Tuesday	…………………..	………………….
Wednesday	…………………..	………………….
Thursday	…………………..	………………….
Friday	…………………..	………………….
Saturday	…………………..	………………….

Exercise 8: Draw the time written below:

الثامنة وعَشر

ath-thaamena wa Aashr

العاشِرَة وثُلُث

al-Aaashera wa thuluth

الخامِسَة إلا رُبع

al-khaamesa il-laa rubA

الثانية وخَمس

ath-thaanya wa khams

الرَابِعَة إلا ثُلُث

ar-raabeAa il-laa thuluth

الخامِسَة إلا عَشَر

al-khaamesa il-laa Aashar

Exercise 9: Write down the time in Arabic below the pictures:

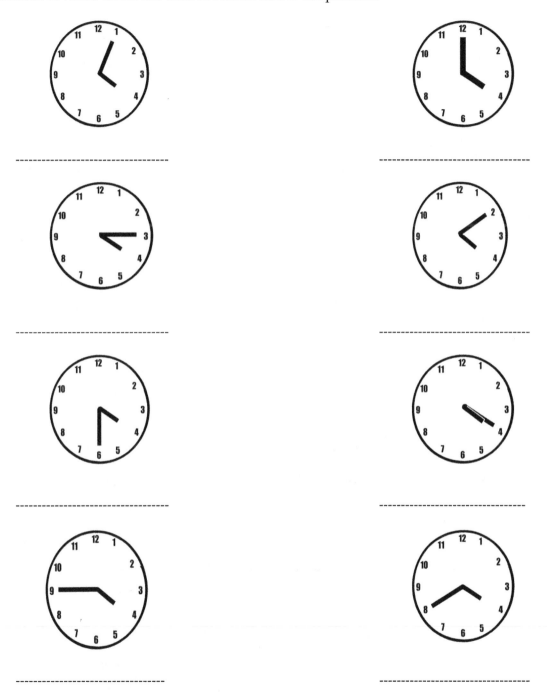

Exercise 10: What does it mean?

English	Transliteration	Arabic
....	Daabet	ضابِط
....	Aalaa Tuul	عَلَى طُول
....	jaaneb	جَانِب
....	Alet-tejaahaat	الاتّجاهات
....	maHaT-TaT qetaar	مَحطّة قِطار
....	funduq	فُنْدُق
....	maktab el-bariid	مَكْتَب البَريد
....	kam Tuul	كَم طول
....	eshaarat muruur	إشارة مُرور
....	masaafa	مَسافَة
....	yamiin	يَمين
....	shemaal / yasaar	شِمال / يَسار
....	maTaar	مَطار

Vocabulary

front of, أمام
'amaam

behind, وَراء
waraa'

right, يَمين
yamiin

left, شِمال / يَسار
shemaal / yasaar

straight / ahead, عَلى طُول
Aalaa Tuul

side, جانِب
jaaneb

directions, اتّجاهات
et-tejaahaat

street, شارِع
shariiA

road, طَريق
Tariiq

station, مَحَطَّة
maHaT-Ta

petrol station, مَحَطَّة بَنْزين
maHaT-TaT banziin

building, بِناية
benaaya

hotel, فُنْدُق
funduq

museum, مَتْحَف
matHaf

post office, مَكْتَب البَريد
maktab el-bariid

How long, كَم طُول
kam Tuul

traffic light, إشارة مُرور
eshaarat muruur

distance, مَسافة
masaafa

airport, مَطار
maTaar

you (formal), حَضْرة
HaDret

train, قِطار

The first, الأوَّل
al-'aw-wal

The second, الثّاني
ath-thaanii

The third, الثّالِث
ath-thaaleth

The fourth, الرّابِع
ar-raabeA

The fifth, الخامِس
al-khaames

The sixth, السّادِس
as-saades

The seventh, السّابِع
as-saabeA

The eighth, الثّامِن
ath-thaamen

The ninth, التّاسِع
at-taaseA

The tenth, العاشِر
al-Aaasher

The eleventh, الحادِي عَشَر
al-Hadii Aashar

The twelfth, الثّاني عَشَر
ath-thaanii Aashar

hour, ساعة
saaAa

day, يوم
yawm

minute / minutes, دَقيقَة / دَقائِق
daqeeqa / daqaa'eq

week / weeks, أسْبوع / أسابيع
'asbuuA / 'asaabeeA

month / months, شَهْر / شُهور
shahr / shuhuur

year / years, سَنَة / سنين
sana / seniin

century / centuries, قَرْن / قُرون
qarn / quruun

time, وَقْت
waqt

quarter, رُبْع

qeTaar

truck, شاحِنة

shaaHena

car, سَيّارة

say-yaara

ship, سَفينة

safiina

aircraft, طائِرة

Taa'era

bus, حافِلة

Haafela

zero, صِفر

Sefr

one, واحِد

waHed

two, اثنان / اِثْنَين

'ethnaan/'ethnayn

three, ثَلاثَة

thalatha

four, أرْبَعة

'arbaAa

five, خَمْسة

khamsa

six, سِتّة

set-ta

seven, سَبْعة

sabAa

eight, ثَمانية

thamaaneya

nine, تِسْعة

tesAa

ten, عَشَرة

Aashara

rubA

third, ثُلُث

thuluth

Less: literally: except, إلّا-

il-la

a second, ثانية

thanya

usually, عادةً

Aadatan

sometimes, أحياناً

'aHyaanan

always, دائما

daa'eman

rarely, نادرا

naaderan

immediately, حالاً

Haalan

after, بَعد

baAd

before, قَبْل

qabl

Sunday, يَوْم الأحَد

yawm el-'aHad

Monday, يَوْم الاُثْنَين

yawm el-ethnayn

Tuesday, يَوْم الثُّلاثاء

yawm ethulathaa'

Wednesday, يَوْم الأرْبعاء

yawm el-arbeAa'

Thursday, يَوْم الخَميس

yawm el-khamees

Friday, يَوْم الجُمعَة

yawm el-jumuAa

Saturday, يَوْم السَّبْت

yawm as-sabt

Visit the book website to find out more!
http://www.LetsTalkArabic.com

UNIT EIGHT

At the Supermarket?

UNIT EIGHT

At the Supermarket?

Contents

- Dialogue

- Vocabulary

- Culture notes

- Grammar usage

  IDaafa Possession Construction

- Exercises

فِي السُّوق (السُّوبر مارْكِت)

fes-souq (es-super market)

Dialogue: Sara went to the supermarket to buy some of her needs.

English	Transliteration	Arabic
Sara: Excuse me, where can I find the cheese, please?	*A: : Aafwan, 'ayn 'ajed al-jubn men faDlek.*	**سارة**: عَفوَاً، أين أجِد الجُبْن مِن فَضْلِك.
Clerk: Yes miss, it's there in the dairy section, at the end of this corridor.	*C: naAm ya anesa; hunaak fii qesm el'albaan fii 'akher haTHaa al-mamar.*	**المُوَظّف**: نَعَم يا آنسة؛ هُناك في قِسْم الألْبان؛ في آخِر هَذا المَمَرّ.
Sara: Thanks.	*A: shukran.*	**سارة**: شُكْراً.
Clerk: Is there anything else you want?	*C: hal turiidiin 'ay shay' akhar?*	**المُوَظّف**: هَلْ تُريدينَ أيّ شَيْء آخَر؟
Sara: Yes, can you also tell me where to find the shampoo?	*A: naAam. hal men l-mumken 'an taquul lii 'ayDan 'ayn ash-shaampuu?*	**سارة**: نعم؛ هَلْ مِن المُمْكِن أنْ تَقول لي أيْضاً أيْن الشّامبو؟
Clerk: Sure, it's at the health and beauty supplies in aisle 4.	*C: 'akiid. Aend rukn alAenaaya beS-SeHa wa 'adawaat at-tajmiil fii almamar 4.*	**الموظف**: أكيد. عِنْد رُكْن العِنايَة بالصّحَة وأدَوات التّجْميل في المَمَرّ 4.
Sara: Thanks a lot.	*A: Shukran jed-dan.*	**سارة**: شُكْراً جِداً.
Clerk: You're welcome, have a nice day.	*C: nahaarek saAiid.*	**المُوَظّف**: نَهارك سَعيد.

Vocabulary

English	Transliteration	Arabic
butter	zobd	زُبْد
	uHeb az-zobd Aalaa lfuTuur	أحب الزبد على الفُطور
first	'aw-wal	أَوّل
	al-'aHad huwa 'aw-wal yawm fil-'ausbooA al'Aarabyy	الأحد هو أول يوم في الأسبوع العربي
end / last	'akher	آخِر
	'askun fii 'akher haThaa ash-shaareA	أسكن في آخر هذا الشارع
I find	'ajed	أَجِد
	'ayn 'ajed alketaab? fil-maktaba	أين أجد الكتاب؟ في المكتبة
possible	mumken	مُمْكِن
bread	khubz	خُبْز
	mumken khubz men faDlek	مُمكِن خُبز مِن فضلك!
Is it possible to	hal men-l-mumken	هَلْ مِن المُمْكِن؟
cheese	jubn	جُبْن
	uHeb aljubn Aalaa al-Aashaa'	أحب الجبن على العشاء
clerk	muwaTH-THaf	مُوَظّف
department / section	qesm	قِسْم

dairy	'albaan	آلْبان
'ayn qesm al-'albaan men faDlek?		أين قسم الألبان من فضلك؟
corridor / aisle	mamar	مَمَرّ
ilaa 'ayna yaThhab haThaa almamar		إلى أين يذهب هذا الممر؟
anything	'ayy shay'	أيّ شَيْء
I want	uriid	أُريد
else	'akhar	آخَر
hal turiid 'ayy shay's 'akhar?		هل تُريد أي شيء آخَر؟
beauty	tajmiil	تجْميل
corner	rukn	رُكْن
supplies	'adawaat	أدَوات
'ayn rkn 'adawaat at-tajmiil?		أين رُكن أدوات التجميل؟
happy / nice day	nahaar saAiid	نهار سَعيد
health	aS-SeHa	الصّحَة
kayf aS-SeHa? bekhayr shukran		كيف الصحة؟ بخير شكراً
nahaarak sAiid		نهارك سعيد

N	Transliteration	Arabic	N
1	khas	خَسْ	1
2	jazar	جَزر	2
3	kheyaar	خِيار	3
4	qarnabiiT	قَرنبيط	4
5	baSal	بَصَل	5
6	khuDaar (Vegetables)	خُضار	6
7	baThenjaan	باذِنجان	7
8	zanjabiil	زَنْجَبيل	8
9	malfouf /kurunb	مَلفوف / كُرُنب	9
10	TamaaTem	طَماطِم	10
11	kurunb 'aHmar	كُرُنب أحْمَر	11
12	broukly	بروكلي	12
13	baazel-laa'	بازِلّاء	13

N	Transliteration	Arabic	N
1	*jwaafa*	جَوافة	1
2	*tuf-faaH*	تفّاح	2
3	*Aenab*	عِنَب	3
4	*sham-maam*	شَمّام	4
5	*'anaanaas*	أناناس	5
6	*mouz*	موز	6
7	*burtuqaal*	بُرْتُقال	7
8	*tuf-faaH*	تُفّاح	8
9	*laymoun*	لَيْمون	9
10	*rum-maan*	رُمّان	10
11	*Aenab*	عِنَب	11
12	*tiin*	تِين	12
13	*faraawlah*	قَراولَة	13
14	*kum-methraa*	كُمّثَرَى	14

N	Transliteration	Arabic	N
1	faTiira / bitza	فَطيرة / بيتزا	1
2	shaTiira	شَطيرة	2
3	laHm	لَحْم	3
4	dajaaj	دَجاج	4
5	khubz	خُبْز	5
6	jubn	جُبْن	6
7	baTaaTes	بَطاطِس	7
8	fawaakeh	فَواكِه	8
9	bayD	بَيْض	9
10	zaytoun	زَيْتون	10

Fill in the blanks with one of the new Vocabulary

1- 'askun fii .... fii haTha ash-shaareA.

١- أسكن في .... في هذا الشارع.

2- 'ayn .... az-zubd wal-jubn men fadDlek?

٢- أين .... الزّبد والجُبن من فضلك؟

3- .... 'an taquul lii 'ayn al-khubz?

٣- .... أن تقول لي أين الخُبز؟

4- 'ayn .... al'albaan men faDlek?

٤- أين .... الألبان من فضلك؟

5- 'adawaat at-tajmiil hunaak fii 'akher haThaa al ....

٥- أدوات التجميل هناك في آخِر هذا الـ ....

6- hal turiid .... 'akhar men as-suuq?

٦- هل تُريد .... آخَر من السـوق؟

7- lii Sadiiq yaAmal .... fil-bank alAarabyy.

٧- لي صديق يعمل .... في البنك العربي.

Say it in Arabic

1- My friend is an employee here

2- I'm going to the market, do you want anything from there?

3- Do you work in the Arabic department?

4- I like to eat bread with cheese for breakfast

5- I live at the end of this street

6- I'm always the first one at work

7- Where can I find the fruit please?

Culture Notes

Like most of the cultures all over the world, it is a common practice in Arabic Culture that when you want to ask someone about something, you start the conversation by saying "excuse me" *Aafwan* عفواً. If you want to ask somebody for his or her permission before asking something, before leaving or to finish the conversation, you can say بعد إذنـك/*baAd iThnak/ik* = excuse me, as it's considered rude to leave without saying anything.

الإضافة

IDaafa

Possession

One of the essential structures of Arabic is (*IDaafa*) which consists of two or more nouns are put together to make a possession. For example:

اِبن العَم	بِنْت الأخ	اِبْن الأخ
ebn el-Aamm	*bent el-'akh*	*ebn el-'akh*
سيّارة آدَم	كِتاب سارة	بنت الخال
say-yaarat 'adam	*ketaab saara*	*bent el-khaal*
عائِلَة الوالد	جامِعَة الأزْهَر	مَدينَة القاهرة
Aaa'elat el-waaled	*jaameAat el-azhar*	*madiinat el-qaahera*

1- Remember that (*IDaafa*) equal in English when you say (in literal translation) :

Son of the brother	Daughter of the brother	Son of the uncle
Daughter of the uncle	Book of Sara	Car of Adam
City of Cairo	University of Al-Azhar	Family of the father

2-Just the last word in (*IDaafa*) can take the article (*al*) or a passive suffix, like;

جامِعَة العين	مكتب الرئيس	عائِلة والدي
jaameAat el-Ayn	*maktab er-ra'iis*	*Aa'elat waaledy*
بِنت أختي	رِسالة أخي	نِمْرَة تليفوني
bent ukhty	*resaalat 'akhy*	*nemrat -telephouny*

3-For *IDaafa* in spoken Arabic you can observe the (*Ta' marbuuta*) which is the last letter and we pronounce it as (a) is pronounced as normal *taa'* as in:

جامِعَة العين
jaameAat el-Ayn
University of Al-Ayn

عائِلة والدي
Aa'elat waaledy
The family of my father

رِسالة أخي
resaalat 'akhy
The message of my brother

نِمْرة تليفوني
nemrat -telephouny
The number of my phone

Exercise 1: Match each word in (**A**) with an appropriate word in (**B**) to make a useful *IDaafa*:

B

'akhii	أخي
Aam-mii	عَمّي
ukhtii	أختي
Sadiiqatii	صديقتي
as-salaam	السَلامُ
al-maktab	المَكْتب
telefuunii	تليفوني
al-lughaat	اللُغات
'aBuu THaby	أبوظبي
waaledatii	والدتي

A

ghurfat	غُرفة
bayt	بيت
ebn	اِبن
bint	بِنت
ebn	اِبْن
Aaa'elat	عائِلَة
shaarA	شارِع
raqam	رَقم
kul-ly-yat	كلية
jaameAat	جامِعة

Exercise 2: Translate into Arabic

1- Excuse me. Where can I find the water, please?

....

2- Where is the chicken/ beef / fish please?

....

3- It's at the end of this corridor.

....

4- Excuse me/ pardon!

....

5- Can you tell me please where can I find the sugar?

....

6- Do you want anything else?

....

7- Have a nice day.

....

8- This is Sara's car.

....

9- Where is Cairo University please?

....

10- What's your phone number?

....

11- My nephew is a student in Arabic school.

....

12- My niece is a student in a school of girls.

....

Exercise 3: Can you write them in Arabic?

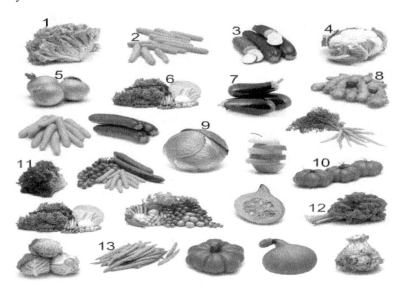

N	Transliteration	Arabic	N
1	....	....	1
2	....	....	2
3	....	....	3
4	....	....	4
5	....	....	5
6	....	....	6
7	....	....	7
8	....	....	8
9	....	....	9
10	....	....	10
11	....	....	11
12	....	....	12
13	....	....	13

Exercise 4: Can you write them in Arabic?

N	Transliteration	Arabic	N
1	………………………………..	………………………………..	1
2	………………………………..	………………………………..	2
3	………………………………..	………………………………..	3
4	………………………………..	………………………………..	4
5	………………………………..	………………………………..	5
6	………………………………..	………………………………..	6
7	………………………………..	………………………………..	7
8	………………………………..	………………………………..	8
9	………………………………..	………………………………..	9
10	………………………………..	………………………………..	10
11	………………………………..	………………………………..	11
12	………………………………..	………………………………..	12
13	………………………………..	………………………………..	13
14	………………………………..	………………………………..	14

Exercise 5: What does it mean?

اِبْن الأخ	بِنْت الأخ	اِبِن العَم
ebn el-'akh	bent el-'akh	ebn el-Aamm
....	....	....

بنت الخال	كِتاب سارة	سيّارة آدَم
bent el-khaal	ketaab saara	say-yaarat 'adam
....	....	....

مَدينَة القاهرة	جامِعَة الأزْهَر	عائِلَة الوالد
madiinat el-qaahera	jaameAat el-azhar	Aaa'elat el-waaled
....	....	....

عائِلة والدي	مكتب الرئيس	جامِعَة العين
Aa'elat waaledy	maktab er-ra'iis	jaameAat el-Ayn
....	....	....

نِمْرَة تليفوني	رسالة أخي	بنت أختي
nemrat –telephouny	resaalat 'akhy	bent ukhty
....	....	....

Exercise 6: Conjugate the verbs below in present tense

English	Transliteration	Arabic	Pro
I say	'aquul	أقول	أنا 'anaa
We say	naquul	نَقول	نَحْن naHnu
You say (male)			أنْتَ 'anta
You say (female)			أنْتِ 'anti
You say (plural)			أنتم 'antum
He says			هُوَ huwa
She says			هِيَ heya
They say			هُمْ hum

English	Transliteration	Arabic	Pro
I find	*'ajed*	أجِد	أنا *'anaa*
We find	*najed*	نَجِد	نَحْن *naHnu*
You find (male)			أنْتَ *'anta*
You find (female)			أنْتِ *'anti*
You find (plural)			أنتم *'antum*
He finds			هُوَ *huwa*
She finds			هِيَ *heya*
They find			هُمْ *hum*

Exercise 7: Match the balloon with the meaning

possible

last / end

I find

first

else

department / section

corner

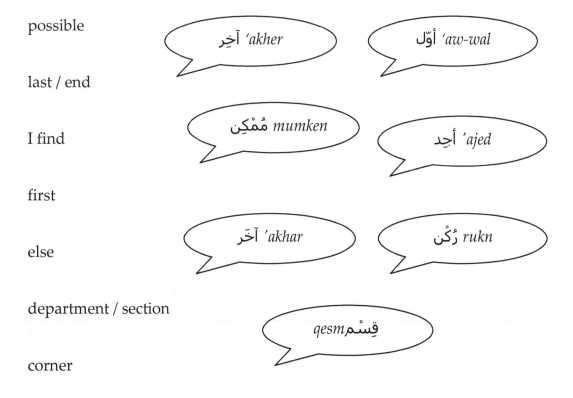

Exercise 8: Fill in the blanks using the vocabulary you have learned, to make a dialogue

Sara: Excuse me, where can I find the butter, please?

A:..........................

سارة:....................

....

....

Clerk: It's there in the dairy section, at the end of this corridor.

C:........................

المُوَظّف:...................

....

....

Sara: Thanks.

A: ....

سارة: شُكْراً.

Exercise 9: Write down a list of things you want to buy from the supermarket

1- ....   2- ....

3- ....   4- ....

5- ....   6- ....

7- ....   8- ....

9- ....   10- ....

Exercise 10: Can you find the 4 Arabic meanings for the below words in the word square?

1- dairy

2- anything

3- possible

4- supplies

5- health

ي	أ	ل	ب	ا	ن	ر
أ	ي	ش	ي	ء	آ	ز
ك	ن	م	م	ك	ن	ى
ع	أ	د	و	ا	ت	ف
ق	ح	ا	ل	ص	ح	ة

Vocabulary

butter, زُبْد
zobd

first, أوّل
'aw-wal

end / last, آخِر
'akher

I find, أجِد
'ajed

possible (polite request), مُمْكِن
mumken

Is it possible to...?!, هَلْ مِنَ المُمْكِنْ؟!
hal men-l-mumken

cheese, جُبْن
jubn

clerk, مُوَظَّف
muwaTH-THaf

department / section, قِسْم
qesm

dairy, ألْبان
'albaan

corridor / aisle, مَمَرّ
mamar

anything, أيّ شَيْء
'ayy shay'

I want, أريد
uriid

else, آخَر
'akhar

beauty, تجْميل
tajmiil

happy / nice day, نهار سَعيد
nahaar saAiid

health, الصّحّة
aS-SeHa

supplies / tools, أدَوات
'adawaat

corner, رُكْن
rukn

bread, خُبْز
khubz

potatos, بَطاطِس
baTaaTes

tomato, طَماطِم
TamaaTem

Vegetables, خُضار
khuDaar

onion, بَصَل
basal

cucumber, خِيار
kheyaar

lettuce, خَس
khas

carrot, جَزر
jazar

eggplant, بانِنجان
baThenjaan

fruit, فَواكِه
fawaakeh

eggs, بَيْض
bayD

olives, زَيْتون
zaytuun

Visit the book website to find out more!
http://www.LetsTalkArabic.com

UNIT NINE

What happened yesterday

UNIT NINE

What happened yesterday

Contents

- A story

- Vocabulary

- Language notes

- Grammar usage

- Exercises

يَوم صَعْب لِآدَم في الجَامِعَة

yawm SaAb le-'adam fel-jaameAa

A hard day for Adam at the university

Transliteration	Arabic
Kaan yawm l-'aHad yawm SaAb ben-nesba le-'adam.	كان يَوم الأَحَد يَوم صَعْب بالنّسبة لِآدَم؛
Thahab 'elaa l-jaameAa muta'akheran. Le'an-na alHaafela faatat wa lam yalHaq behaa.	ذَهَب إلى الجامِعَة مُتَأَخِّراً؛ لأنّ الحافلة فاتت ولَمْ يَلحق بها.

Sunday was a hard day for Adam. He went to the university late because he missed the bus and he didn't catch it.

faatat 'adam muHaDara muhem-ma. Le'an-nahu SaHa muta'akheran wa waSal 'elaa l-jaameAa baAd aTH-THuhr.	فاتَتْ آدَم مُحاضرة مُهِمّة؛ لِإنه صَحَا مُتَأَخّراً وَوَصل إلى الجامِعَة بَعْد الظّهْر؛
wa Aendamaa dakhal al-muHaaDara ath-thaaneya, kaan al-ustaaTh munzaAejan menhu besabab at-ta'akh-khur. wa le'an-nahu naseya ketaaban haam-man fil-bayt. fa-qad jaa'a bel-Haqiiba alkhaTa'.	وعِنْدَما دَخَل المُحاضرة الثانية؛ كَان الأستاذ مُنْزَعِجا منه بِسَبَب التَأخّر؛ وَلأنّه نَسِيّ كِتاباً هامّاً في البَيت؛ فَقَد جَاءَ بالحَقيبة الخَطَأ.

Adam missed an important lecture, because he woke up late, and reached the university in the afternoon. When he entered the second lecture, the professor was uncomfortable with him because of the delay, and because he had forgotten an important book at home, as he came with the wrong bag.

wa laken-nahu qaal as-sabab lel-ustaaTh. wa leThalek samaHa lahu 'an yadkhul aS-Saf.	وَلكِنه قال السّبَب للأستاذ؛ ولذَلِك سَمَح لَه أنْ يَدْخُل الصّف.

But he said to the professor the reason, so he allowed him to enter the class.

rajaAa 'adam 'elal-bayt baAd al-muHaaDaraat wa huwa zaAlaan jed-dan lemaa Hadath.	رَجَعَ آدَم إلى البَيت بَعْد المُحاضَرات وَهُوَ زَعْلان جِدا لِما حَدَث؛
wa naam mubak-keran le-yaS-Huu qabl mawAed el-jaameAa bewqt kaaf fiS-SabaaH	وَنام مُبَكِّراً لِيصْحو قبل مَوْعِد الجامِعة بوَقت كاف في الصّباح.

Adam came back home after the lectures and he was very upset because of what happened. And he slept early in order to wake up before the university with enough time in the morning.

Vocabulary

English	Transliteration	Arabic
was	*kaan*	كان
yesterday	*ams*	أمس
hard / difficult	*SaAb*	صَعْب
easy	*sahl*	سَهْل
kayf kaan alemteHan ams? sahl 'am SaAb?		كيف كان الامتحان أمس؟ سهل أم صعب؟
for / to / in order to	*Le*	لِ
as for / according to	*ben-nesba le*	بالنّسْبَة لِ
haThaa alkhubz Tay-yeb jed-dan ben-nesba lii		هذا الخُبز طيب جدا بالنسبة لي
went	*Thahab*	ذَهَب
late	*muta'akh-kher*	مُتَأخّر
laa uHeb 'an 'aThhab ilaa alAamal muta'akh-kheran		لا أحب أن أذهب إلى العمل متأخرا
early	*mubak-ker / baaker*	مُبَكّر / باكِر
uHeb 'an 'anaam mubak-keran		أحب أن أنام مبكرا
because	*le'an-na*	لأنّ
laa usaafer bes-say-yaara le'an-na aT-Tariiq Tawiil		لا أسافر بالسيارة لأن الطريق طويل
miss / miss out on	*faat*	فات
catch up	*yalHaq be*	يلحق بـ
did not	*lam*	لَم
faat al-qeTaar wa lam 'alHaq beh		فات القطار ولم ألحق به

important	muhem-m/a	مُهِمّ / ـة
عندي محاضرة مهمة اليوم		*Aendii muHaaDara muhem-ma*
woke up / wake up	SaHaa / yaSHuu	صَحَا / يصحو
sleeping	nawm	نوم
أصحو من النوم الساعة 5 ص		*'asHuu men an-nawm as-saAa 5 Sabahan*
arrived / reached	waSal	وَصَل
وصل القطار متأخرا هذا المساء		*waSal al-qeTaar muta'akheran haThal masaa'*
when	Aendamaa	عِنْدَما
slept	naam	نام
عندما أشرب قهوة ؛ لا أنام جيدا		*Aendamaa 'ashrab qahwa laa 'naam jay-yedan*
afternoon	baAd aTH-THuhr	بَعْد الظّهْر
عندي محاضرة بعد الظهر		*Aendii muHaaDara baAd aTH-THuhr*
entered	dakhal	دَخَل
لا أدخل بيتي قبل الساعة 10 م		*laa 'adkhul baytii qabl as-saAa 10 masaa'an*
because of	be-sabab	بِسَبَب
كان اليوم طويل بسبب الشغل		*kaan alyawm Tawiil besabab ash-shughl*
uncomfortable / mad	munzaAej	مُنزعج
delay	ta'akh-khur	تَأَخُّر
صديقي منزعج بسبب تأخر الحافلة		*Sadiiqii munzaAej be-sabab ta'akh-khur alHaafela*
forgot	naseya	نَسِيَ

naseya aHmad alhaatef fiil bayt		نَسِيَ أحمد الهاتف في البيت
already / may / perhaps	qad	قَدْ
came with / brought	jaa'a be	جاءَ بِ
wrong	khaTa'	خَطَأ
bag	Haqiiba	حَقيبَة
kaan adam qad jaa'a bel-Haqiiba alkhaTa'		كان آدم قد جاء بالحقيبة الخطأ
said	qaal	قال
so	leThalek	لِذَلِك
allow	samaHa le / be	سَمَح لـ / بِ
qaal adam sabab at-ta'akhur lel-ustaaTh, wa leThalek samaHa lahu 'an yadkhul aS-Saf		قال آدم سبب التأخّر للأستاذ؛ ولذلك سمح له أن يدخل الصفّ
came back / returned	rajaA	رَجَع
'arjaA ilaa al-bayt muta'kh-kheran kul yawm		أرجع إلى البيت متأخرا كل يوم
upset	zaAlaan	زَعْلان
hal 'anta zaAlaan maAii? laa		هل أنت زعلان معي؟ لا
happened	Hadath	حَدَث
maaThaa Hadath ams?		ماذا حدث أمس؟
appointment	mawAed	مَوْعِد
sorry	asef / a	آسِف / ــة

Fill in the blanks with one of the new vocabulary

1- kaan al-emteHaan alyawm ....

1- كان الامتحان اليوم ....

2- uHeb Aamalii kathiiran, wa huwa Aamal jay-yed lii

2- أحب عملي كثيرا؛ وهو عمل جَيّد .... لي.

3- .... ilaa almaktab kul yawm ....qabl as-saAa 8.

3- .... إلى المكتب كل يوم .... قبل الساعة 8.

4- nuriid 'an naThhab bes-say-yaara .... albayt baAiid.

4- نُريد أن نذهب بالسيارة .... البيت بعيد.

5- waSal 'akhii ilaa almaHaT-Ta wa kaan al-qeTaar qad ....

5- وصل أخي إلى المحطة متأخرا وكان القطار قد ....

6- uriid 'an 'atakalam maAak fii shay' ....

6- أريد أن أتكلم معك في شيء ....

7- laa .... baytii qabl as-saAa 9 kul yawm.

7- لا .... بيتي قبل الساعة 9 م كل يوم.

Say it in Arabic

1- I'm so busy this week because of work

2- My friend forgot his book at home

3- Are you angry with me?

4- See you in the afternoon because I have a lecture in the morning

5- Sorry for delay

6- I have an appointment in the afternoon

7- I want to sleep early tonight

8- What happened?

9- The test was so easy today

10- I'm not going to work today

Grammar usage

الماضي *al-maaDii*

Past tense

You have seen a few verbs in the above story that express the past tense in Arabic. Note that *al-maaDii = past* in Arabic is conjugated with suffixes. Make it a habit to learn both the present and past tense together. The following chart shows the conjugation of the past tense using the verb **to go**:

English	Transliteration	Arabic	Pro	
I went	*Thahabt(u)*	ذَهَبْتُ	أنا *'anaa*	First person
We went	*Thahabna*	ذَهَبْنَا	نَحْن *naHnu*	
You went (male)	*Thahabt(a)*	ذَهَبْتَ	أنْتَ *'anta*	Second person
You went (female)	*Thahabte*	ذَهَبْتِ	أنْتِ *'anti*	
You went (plural)	*Thahabtum*	ذَهَبْتُم	أنتم *'antum*	
He went	*Thahab(a)*	ذَهَبَ	هُوَ *huwa*	Third person
She went	*Thahabat*	ذَهَبَتْ	هِيَ *heya*	
They went	*Thahab(uu)*	ذَهَبـوا	هُمْ *hum*	

To conjugate the verb (*kaan* كان)= (he was) remember that it has two stems in conjugation as most of the verbs with the letter (alif) in the middle, they're called (weak verbs). One stem with (alif) for the third persons, and the other one is without (alif)

English	Transliteration	Arabic	Pro	
I was	*kunt(u)*	كُنْتُ	أنا *'anaa*	First person
We were	*kun-na*	كُنّا	نَحْن *naHnu*	
You were (male)	*kunt(a)*	كُنْتَ	أنْتَ *'anta*	second person
You were (female)	*kunte*	كُنْتِ	أنْتِ *'anti*	
You were (plural)	*kuntum*	كُنْتُم	أنتم *'antum*	
He was	*kaan(a)*	كانَ	هُوَ *huwa*	Third person
She was	*kaanat*	كا*نَتْ	هِيَ *heya*	
They were	*kaan(uu)*	كانـوا	هُمْ *hum*	

Negation of the past

You have learned to negate the present with (laa). To negate the past tense in formal Arabic use (maa + the verb in past). For example:

maa kaan = was not = ما كان , *maa Thahaba* = didn't go = ما ذَهَب

To say in past 'said'

English	Transliteration	Arabic	Pro
I said	*qult(u)*	قُلْتُ	أنا *'anaa*
We said	*qulna*	قُلْنا	نَحْن *naHnu*
You said (male)	*qult(a)*	قُلْتَ	أَنْتَ *'anta*
You said (female)	*qulte*	قُلْتِ	أَنْتِ *'anti*
You said (plural)	*qultum*	قُلْتُمْ	أنتم *'antum*
He said	*qaal(a)*	قالَ	هُوَ *huwa*
She said	*qaalat*	قالَتْ	هِيَ *heya*
They said	*qaal(uu)*	قالـوا	هُمْ *hum*

To wake up in past 'woke up'

English	Transliteration	Arabic	Pro
I woke up	*SaHawt(u)*	صَحَوْتُ	أنا *'anaa*
We woke up	*SaHawna*	صَحَوْنا	نَحْن *naHnu*
You woke up (male)	*SaHawt(a)*	صَحَوْتَ	أَنْتَ *'anta*
You woke up (female)	*SaHawte*	صَحَوْتِ	أَنْتِ *'anti*
You woke up (plural)	*SaHawtum*	صَحَوْتُمْ	أنتم *'antum*
He woke up	*SaHa(a)*	صَحَا	هُوَ *huwa*
She woke	*SaHat*	صَحَتْ	هِيَ *heya*
They woke up	*SaHaw(uu)*	صَحَـوا	هُمْ *hum*

Language Notes

You have seen that a few forms with a certain pronouns in the above charts for (*'anaa, 'anta, huwa, hum*) have the suffix written in the transliteration in between brackets, that's to help you to observe that in spoken Arabic most of the Arabic speakers don't pronounce these vowels. For example: they say (*Thahab*) not (*Thahaba*) , and (*Thahabt*) not (*Thahabtu*) without the last vowel.

لِمَ / لِماذا؟

lema / lemaTha? **Why?**

There are four words / phrases to answer the question, "lema? / lemaTha? = why?" in Arabic, or to give information about a reason, each one of them has its grammatical usage:

1- بسبب

be-sabab

On account of / because of

Example:

لا أُحِب هَذا الشّارِع يِسَبَب الزّحام.

*laa uHebb haTha sh-shaareA **be-sabab** ez-zeHaam.*

I don't like this street because of the crowd.

2- عَلَى شَأن / مِن شَأن

Aala sha'n / men sha'n

For the sake of / because of

like the previous word, but used more in spoken language among Arabs, with a lightly fast pronunciation as one word" alashaan" or "menshaan".

Example:

مِن فَضْلك؛ لا تُسْرِع بالسّيارة عَلَى شَأْن الأَوْلاد.

*men faDlek, laa tusreA bes-say-yaara **Aala sha'n** el-'awlaad.*

Please, don't speed up the car, because of the children.

3- لِأَنّ

le'an-na

Because

Example:

أَذْهَب إلى المَكْتَب باكِراً؛ **لِأَنّ** بَيْتي قَريب جِداً.

*aTh-hab elaal maktab baakeran, **le'an-na** baytii qariib jed-dan.*

I go to the office early, because my house is so close.

4- لِ

Le

In order to / for

Examples:

أُحِبّ أَن أُشاهِد التّلفزيون **لِ**لتّسلية.

*uHebb 'an ushaahed et-telfeziuun **le**t-tasleya.*

I like to watch the TV for entertainment.

أَدْرُس اللّغات **لِ**أَتَكَلّم مَعَ النّاس مِن حَوْل العالَم.

*'adrus l-lughaat **le**-'atakal-lam maAa n-naas men Hawl al-Aaalam.*

I study languages in order to speak to people from all over the world.

Exercise 1 : Choose the correct answer for past tense

1- 'adam .... fii madiina saghiira.

١- آدم .... في مَدينة صَغَيرة.

٣- أَسكُن 'askun	سَكَنَ sakana -٢	تَسكُن taskun -١

2- laa .... Dajaaj ya Muhammad

٢- لا............ دجاج يا مُحَمَّد.

تَأكُل ta'akul -٣	تَأكُلي ta'akulii -٢	أَكَلْتَ 'akalta -١

3-'akhii .... Fii jaameAat 'abu dhadi.

٣- أخي .... في جامعة أبوظبي

دَرَسَ darasa -٣	أدْرُس 'adrus -٢	يَدْرُسـون yadrusuun -١

4- 'anaa .... AaSiir burtuqaal.

٤- أنا .... عَصير بُرْثُقال .

يُـريدوا turiiduu -٣	تُريد turiid -٢	شَـرِبْتُ sharebtu -١

5- maaThaa .... yaa kariim.?

٥- ماذا .... يا كريم ؟

تَحبوا tuHebuu -٣	شَـرِبْتَ sharebta -٢	يُـحِب yuHeb -١

6- 'abii .... qahwa fii S-SabaaH.

٦- أبي .... قَهْوَة في الصباح

تَشْرَب tashrab -٣	شَرِبَ shareba -٢	يَـأكُل ya'kul -١

7-...... maAa 'ausratii fii bayt kabiir.

٧- .... مع أسرتي في بيت كبير.

سَكَنتُ sakantu -٣	يَسكُن yaskun -٢	تَسكُن taskun -١

Exercise 2: Conjugate the verbs

English	Transliteration	Arabic	Pro
I was	kunt(u)	كُنْتُ	أنا 'anaa
We were			نَحْن naHnu
You were (male)			أنْتَ 'anta
You were (female)			أنْتِ 'anti
You were (plural)			أنتم 'antum
He was	kaan(a)	كانَ	هُوَ huwa
She was			هِيَ heya
They were			هُمْ hum

English	Transliteration	Arabic	Pro
I said	qult(u)	قُلْتُ	أنا 'anaa
We said			نَحْن naHnu
You said (male)			أنْتَ 'anta
You said (female)			أنْتِ 'anti
You said (plural)			أنتم 'antum
He said	qaal(a)	قالَ	هُوَ huwa
She said			هِيَ heya
They said			هُمْ hum

English	Transliteration	Arabic	Pro
I arrived			أنا 'anaa
We arrived			نَحْن naHnu
You arrived (male)			أنْتَ 'anta
You arrived (female)			أنْتِ 'anti
You arrived (plural)			أنتم 'antum
He arrived	waSala	وَصَل	هُوَ huwa
She arrived			هِيَ heya
They arrived			هُمْ hum

English	Transliteration	Arabic	Pro
I entered			أنا ʻanaa
We entered			نَحْن naHnu
You entered (male)			أنْتَ ʻanta
You entered (female)			أنْتِ ʻanti
You entered (plural)			أنتم ʻantum
He entered	dakhala	دَخَلَ	هُوَ huwa
She entered			هِيَ heya
They entered			هُمْ hum

English	Transliteration	Arabic	Pro
I delayed			أنا ʻanaa
We delayed			نَحْن naHnu
You delayed (male)			أنْتَ ʻanta
You delayed (female)			أنْتِ ʻanti
You delayed (plural)			أنتم ʻantum
He delayed	ta'akh-khara	تَأخَّرَ	هُوَ huwa
She delayed			هِيَ heya
They delayed			هُمْ hum

English	Transliteration	Arabic	Pro
I forgot			أنا ʻanaa
We forgot			نَحْن naHnu
You forgot (male)			أنْتَ ʻanta
You forgot (female)			أنْتِ ʻanti
You forgot (plural)			أنتم ʻantum
He forgot	naseya	نَسِيَ	هُوَ huwa
She forgot			هِيَ heya
They forgot			هُمْ hum

English	Transliteration	Arabic	Pro
I came	je'tu	جِئْتُ	أنا 'anaa
We came			نَحْنُ naHnu
You came (male)			أنْتَ 'anta
You came (female)			أنْتِ 'anti
You came (plural)			أنتم 'antum
He came	jaa'a	جاءَ	هُوَ huwa
She came			هِيَ heya
They came			هُمْ hum

English	Transliteration	Arabic	Pro
I allowed			أنا 'anaa
We allowed			نَحْنُ naHnu
You allowed (male)			أنْتَ 'anta
You allowed (female)			أنْتِ 'anti
You allowed (plural)			أنتم 'antum
He allowed	samaHa	سَمَحَ	هُوَ huwa
She allowed			هِيَ heya
They allowed			هُمْ hum

English	Transliteration	Arabic	Pro
I returned			أنا 'anaa
We returned			نَحْنُ naHnu
You returned (male)			أنْتَ 'anta
You returned(female)			أنْتِ 'anti
You returned (plural)			أنتم 'antum
He returned	rajaAa	رَجَعَ	هُوَ huwa
She returned			هِيَ heya
They returned			هُمْ hum

English	Transliteration	Arabic	Pro
I slept	*nemt(u)*	نِمْتُ	أنا 'anaa
We slept			نَحْن naHnu
You slept (male)			أنْتَ 'anta
You slept (female)			أنْتِ 'anti
You slept (plural)			أنتم 'antum
He slept	*naama*	نامَ	هُوَ huwa
She slept			هِيَ heya
They slept			هُمْ hum

Exercise 3: Translate into Arabic

1- Did you live in Qatar? [Male, female, plural]

………………………………………………………………

2-I lived and worked in Qatar.

………………………………………………………………

3- I drank coffee in the morning.

………………………………………………………………

4- Did you order?

………………………………………………………………

5- Did you eat Arabic food?

………………………………………………………………

6- She woke up late today.

………………………………………………………………

7- We ate Arabic food yesterday.

………………………………………………………………

8- I studied Arabic language in the school.

………………………………………………………………

9-They were here just now.

………………………………………………………………

Exercise 4: Conjugate the below verbs on outside worksheet

English	Transliteration	Arabic
he knew	Aarafa	عَرَفَ
he understood	fahema	فَهِمَ
he heard	sameAa	سَمِعَ
he read	qara'a	قَرَأَ
he sat	jalasa	جَلَسَ
he went out	kharaja	خَرَجَ
he watched	shaahada	شاهَدَ
he traveled	saafara	سافَرَ

Exercise 5: Match the word with its meaning

hard / difficult	mubak-ker/baaker	مُبَكّر / باكِر
easy	le'an-na	لأنّ
to / in order to	muhem/ma	مُهِمّ / ـة
as for / according to	Aendamaa	عِنْدَما
late	baAd aTH-THuhr	بَعْد الظّهْر
early	SaAb	صَعْب
because	sahl	سَهْل
important	Le	لِ
when	ben-nesba le	بالنّسْبَة لِ
afternoon	muta'akh-kher	مُتَأخّر
uncomfortable	leThalek	لِذَلِك
because of	zaAlaan	زَعْلان
so	munzaAej	مُنْزعج
upset	be-sabab	بِسَبَب

Exercise 6: What does it mean?

....	'ayn kunta?	أيْنَ كُنْتَ؟
....	'ayn kunte?	أيْنَ كُنتِ؟
....	'ayn kuntum?	أين كُنْتُمْ؟
....	kayf kaana yamuka?	كَيف كان يومك؟
....	kayf kaana 'ams?	كيف كان أمس؟
....	kayf kaanat al-muHaaDara?	كيف كانت المحاضرة؟

Exercise 7: Translate into English

Transliteration	Arabic
Kaan yawm l-'aHad yawm SaAb ben-nesba le-'adam.	كان يَوم الأَحَد يَوم صَعْب بالنّسبة لِآدَم؛
Thahab 'elaa l-jaameAa muta'akheran. Le'an-na alHaafela faatat wa lam yalHaq behaa.	ذَهَب إلى الجامِعَة مُتَأَخِّراً؛ لأنّ الحافلة فاتت ولَمْ يَلحق بها.
....	....
....	....

Exercise 8: Write down seven sentences in Arabic about what did you do yesterday!

1- ....
2- ....
3- ....
4- ....
5- ....
6- ....
7- ....

Exercise 9: Can you find the 4 Arabic meanings for the below words in the word square?

1- mad

2- because of

3- because

4- delay

5- forgot

ي	م	ن	ز	ع	ج	ر
أ	ب	س	ب	ب	آ	ز
ك	ل	أ	نّ	ر	أ	ى
ت	أ	خ	ر	ي	ر	ف
ق	ن	س	ي	آ	ن	و

Exercise 10: Using the words below, fill in the puzzle with the meanings. Remember to go from right to left or up to down.

Down

2- he went

4- because

Across

1- so

3- he arrived

5- because of

VOCABULARY

hard / difficult, صَعْب
SaAb

easy, سَهْل
sahl

for / to / in order to, لِـ
Le

as for / according to, بِالنِّسْبَة لِـ
ben-nesba le

he went, ذَهَب
Thahab

late, مُتَأَخِّر
muta'akh-kher

early, مُبَكِّر / باكِر
mubak-ker / baaker

because, لِأَنّ
le'an-na

miss / miss out on / passed, فات
faat

catch up, يَلحَق بِـ
yalHaq be

important, مُهِمّ / ة
muhem/ma

he woke up, صَحَا
SaHaa

he arrived / reached, وَصَل
waSal

when (not for questions), عِنْدَما
Aendamaa

afternoon, بَعْد الظُّهْر
baAd aTH-THuhr

he entered, دَخَل
dakhal

he was, كان
kaan

uncomfortable / mad, مُنْزَعِج
munzaAej

because of, بِسَبَب
be-sabab

delay, تَأَخُّر
ta'akh-khur

he forgot, نَسِيَ
naseya

already / may / perhaps, قَدْ
qad

came with / brought, جاءَ بِـ
jaa'a be

wrong, خَطَأ
khaTa'

correct, صحيح
Sahiih

bag, حَقيبة
Haqiiba

he said, قال
qaal

so / therefore, لِذَلِك
leThalek

allow, سَمَح لِـ / بِـ
samaHa le / be

came back / returned, رَجَع
rajaA

upset, زَعْلان
zaAlaan

happened, حَدَث
Hadath

he slept, نام
naam

appointment, مَوْعِد
mawAed

sorry, آسِف
asef

yesterday, أمس
ams

UNIT TEN

Going Shopping

UNIT TEN

Going Shopping

Contents

- Dialogue: Going Shopping

- Vocabulary

- Culture notes

- Colors

- Grammar usage

- Exercises

Going Shopping

التَّسَوُّق

At-tasaw-wuq

English	Transliteration	Arabic
Clerk: Welcome. How can I help you?	*C: 'ahlan wa sahlan. 'ayy khedma?*	المُوَظّف: أَهْلاً وَسَهْلاً. أَيّ خِدمَة؟
Sara: Thanks, I'd like just to have a look first.	*S: shukran. 'awadd 'an 'ulqii naTHra aw-walan faqaT.*	سارة: شُكْراً؛ أَوَدّ أن أُلْقي نَظْرَة أولاً فقط.
Clerk: There's a sale on everything in this Dept today.	*C: hunaak khuSoumaat Aalaa kul shay' fii haThaa al-qesm alyawm.*	المُوَظّف: هُناك خُصُومَات عَلَى كُلّ شَيْء في هَذا القِسْم اليَوم.
	Ten Minutes later	
Sara: Can I try this sweater on, please?	*S: hal men al-mumken 'an 'ujar-reb qeyaas haThehe es-sutra men faDlek?*	ساره: هل مِنْ المُمْكِن أن أَجَرّب قِياس هَذِهِ السُّتْرة مِنْ فَضْلِك؟
Clerk: Certainly. The fitting room is over there.	*C: bet-ta'kiid. ghurfat alqeyaas hunaak.*	المُوَظّف: بالتّأكيد. غُرْفة القِياس هُناك.

Two minutes later

Clerk: How is the size?	*C: kayf al-maqaas?*	**المُوَظَّف**:كَيْف المَقاسْ؟
Sara: I think it's big, have you got a smaller size?	*S: 'aTHun 'an-nahaa kabiira, hal Aendak maqaas 'aSghar?*	**سارة**: أَظُنّ أَنَّها كَبيرة؛ هَلْ عِنْدك مَقاس أصْغَر؟
Clerk: I have. But with different colors!	*C: Aendii, wa laken be'alwaan mukhtalefa.*	**المُوَظَّف**: عِنْدي؛ وَلكِن بِأَلْوَان مُخْتَلِفة.
Sara: Which colors do you have?	*S: 'ayy 'alwaan Aendak?*	**سارة**: أي أَلْوان عِندك؟
Clerk: Blue, black and white.	*C: al'azraq wal'aswad wa al'abyaD.*	**المُوَظَّف**: الأَزرق والأَسْوَد والأَبْيَض.

Sara: I will take the black one.	S: 'akhuTh el'aswad.	سارة: آخُذ الأسْوَد.
Clerk: Here you are.	C: tafaD-Dalii.	المُوَظّف: تَفَضّلي.
Sara: Thank you.	S: shukran.	سارة: شُكْرَاً.

Vocabulary

English	Transliteration	Arabic
shopping	tasaw-wuq	تَسَوُّق
	uriid 'an 'aThhab let-tasaw-wuq	أريد أن أذهب للتسوق
I have a look	ulqii naTHra	ألقي نَظْرة
first	aw-walan	أوَّلاً
	hal yumken 'an ulqii naTHra aw-walan	هل يُمكن أن ألُقي نظرة أولا
sale	khaSm	خَصْم
everything	kul shay'	كُلْ شَيْء
	hunaak khaSm Aalaa kul shay' el-yawm	هناك خصم على كل شيء اليوم
sweater	sutra	سُتْرَة
dress	fustaan	فُستان
shirt	qamiiS	قَمِيص

194

suit	*badlah*	بَدْلة
pants	*banTaluun*	بَنْطَلون
scarf	*TarHa*	طَرحة
socks	*jawaaareb*	جَوارب

uriid haThehe es-sutra, wa haThaa lqamiiS wal banTaluun, wal badla, wa haThaal fustaan wa huThehe eT-TurIIu waljuwaareb

أريد هذه السُترة؛ وهذا القميص والبنطلون؛ والبدلة؛ وهذا الفستان؛ وهذه الطرحة والجوارب

tie	*rabTat Aunuq*	ربطة عُنُق
how much?	*bekam?*	بِكَم؟

bekam rabTat al-Aunuq

بكم ربطة العنق؟

certainly	*bet-ta'kiid*	بالتّأكيد
fitting room	*ghurfat al-qeyaas*	غُرفَة القِياس
I try	*ujar-reb*	أجرّب

hal yumken 'an ujar-reb haThaa? naAam bet-ta'kiid, ghurfat al-qeyaas hunaak

هل يمكن أن أُجَرّب هذا؟ نعم بالتأكيد؛ غُرفة القياس هناك

large	*waseA/a*	واسِع / ـة
tight	*Day-yeq/a*	ضَيْق / ـة
I think	*'aThun*	أظنّ

195

'aThun 'an haThaa l-qamiiS Day-yeq, uriid al-qamiiS al-waaseA

أظن أن هذا القميص ضيق؛ أريد القميص الواسع

size	almaqaas	المَقاسْ
different	mukhtalef/a	مُخْتَلِف/ـة
colors	'alwaan	ألْوان
bigger	'akbar	أكبر
smaller	'aSghar	أصغر

hal Aendakum maqaas 'akbar? be'alwaan mukhtalefa?

هل عندكم مقاس أكبر؟ بألوان مختلفة؟

big	kabiir/a	كَبِيرة/ة
small	Saghiir/a	صَغِيرة/ة
blue	'azraq	آزْرَق
black	'aswad	أسْوَد
white	'abyaD	أبَيَض
clothes	malaabes	مَلابِس

uHeb el-malaabes al-Aaraby-ya

أحَب الملابس العربية

Say it in Arabic

1- I always go shopping on Friday

2- May I have a look first please?

3- There is a huge discount on everything today in the market

4- May I see this sweater please? certainly

5- I like this shirt, but what colors do you have?

6- Where is the fitting room please?

7- I have the same suit, but with different color

8- These trousers are good but a bit tight

9- I like these clothes

10- Can I have the black?

Fill in the blanks with one of the new Vocabulary

1- hal tuHeb 'an naThhab le................ alyawm baAd aTh-Thuhr?

١- هل تحب أن نذهب لـ .... اليوم بعد الظهر؟

2- hunaak .... Aalaa kul shay' elyawm fii as-suuq.

٢- هناك .... على كل شيء اليوم في السوق.

3- haThaa albanTaluun ...., hal Aendak maqaas 'akbar?

٣- هذا البنطلون ....؛ هل عندك مقاس أكبر؟

4- hal Aendakum 'alwaan ....?

٤- هل عندكم ألوان ....؟

5- haThehe elbadla waaseAa, hal Aendakum maqaas ....?

٥- هذه البدلة واسعة؛ هل عندكم مقاس ....؟

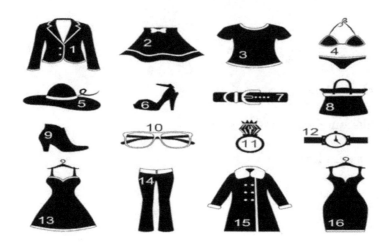

N	Transliteration	Arabic	N
1	*sutra*	سُتْرَة	1
2	*tan-noura*	تَنّورة	2
3	*tiishiirt*	تي شيرت	3
4	*biikiiny*	بيكيني	4
5	*qub-baAa*	قُبّعَة	5
6	*kaAb Aalii*	كَعْب عالي	6
7	*Hezaam*	حِزام	7
8	*Haqiiba*	حَقيبة	8
9	*HeThaa'*	حِذاء	9
10	*naTH-THaara*	نَظّارة	10
11	*khaatam*	خاتَم	11
12	*saaAa*	ساعَة	12
13	*fustaan*	فُستان	13
14	*serwaal*	سيروال	14
15	*meATaf*	مِعْطَف	15

N	Transliteration	Arabic	N
1	qamiss	قَميص	1
2	qub-baAa	قُبّعة	2
3	tiishiirt	تي شيرت	3
4	koufey-ya	كوفيّة	4
5	HeThaa'	حِذاء	5
6	malaabes daakhley-ya	ملابِس داخليّة	6
7	naTH-THaara	نَظّارة	7
8	HeThaa' ryaaDii	حِذاء رِياضي	8
9	sutra	سُترة	9
10	serwaal	سِروال	10
11	meATaf	مِعْطَف	11
13	kaab	كاب	13
14	Heaam	حِزام	14
15	Haqiiba	حَقيبة	15
16	saaAa	ساعة	16

Culture Notes

Colors in the Arab world are also used to describe the persons or sometimes the good and the bad events in our life. For example *yawm 'aswad* = black day for a bad day, or *yawm 'abyaD* = white day for a good day.

Colors

الألْوَان *al-'alwaan*

There are two types of color adjectives in Arabic. The first type consists of adjectives derived from nouns, which have the same form as the adjectives of nationalities.

Here are some common adjectives of this type

Masculine singular	Feminine singular	Color
زَهْري *zahryy*	زَهْرِيّة *zahrey-ya*	Pink
بُرْتُقالي *burtuqaalyy*	بُرْتُقالية *burtuqaaly-ya*	Orange
بُنّي *bun-nyy*	بُنية *bun-ney-ya*	Brown
فِضّي *feD-Dyy*	فِضّية *feD-Dy-ya*	Silver
ذَهَبي *Thahabyy*	ذَهَبِيّة *Thahabey-ya*	Gold

The second type of color words in a certain form for singular feminine and masculine as well.

Masculine singular	Feminine singular	Color
أَبْيَض 'abyaD	بَيْضاء bayDaa'	White
أَسْوَد 'aswad	سَوْداء sawdaa'	Black
أَحْمَر 'aHmar	حَمْراء Hamraa'	Red
أَصْفَر 'aSfar	صَفْراء Safraa'	Yellow
أَخْضَر 'akhDar	خَضْراء khaDraa'	Green
أَزْرَق 'azraq	زَرْقاء zarqaa'	Blue

Exercise 1: Translate into Arabic:

1- My sister has a blue sweater.

....

2- I like the green color.

....

3- Omar likes to write with the red pen.

....

4- Kareem is a very good man, his heart [qalbuhu قلبه] is white.

....

5- I have a white shirt.

....

Exercise 2: Guess the meaning to learn new words:

A- The Red Cross means.........................

الصّليب الأحمر	الصليب الأزرق	الصليب الأسود
1-aS-Saliib al-aHmar	2- aS-Saliib al-azraq	3- aS-Saliib al'aswad

B- The Red Crescent means ....

الهلال الأحمر	الهلال الأزرق	الهلال الأسود
1-al-helaal al-aHmar	2- al-helaal al-azraq	3- a-helaal al'aswad

C- Yellow pages means ....

صَفحات زرقاء	صَفحات صَفْراء	صَفحات بُنيّة
1-SafHaat zarqaa'	2-SafHaat Safraa'	3- SafHaat bun-ny-ya

D- Blue Sky means ....

سَماء زرقاء	سَماء بيضاء	سَماء بُنيّة
1-samaa' zarqaa'	2-samaa' bayDaa'	3- samaa' bun-ny-ya

Exercise 3: Conjugate the following verbs in present tense

English	Transliteration	Arabic
I wear	'albas	أَلْبَس
I take off	'akhlaA	أَخْلَع
I buy	'ashtarii	أشْتري
I look	'anTHur	أنْظُر
I'd like	'awad-d	أوَدّ

Exercise 4: Can you write them in Arabic?

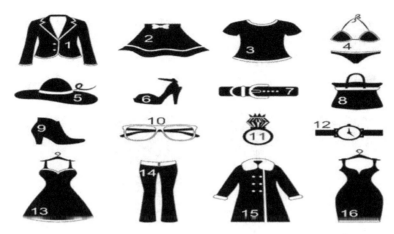

N	Transliteration	Arabic	N
1	....	....	1
2	....	....	2
3	....	....	3
4	....	....	4
5	....	....	5
6	....	....	6
7	....	....	7
8	....	....	8
9	....	....	9
10	....	....	10
11	....	....	11
12	....	....	12
13	....	....	13
14	....	....	14
15	....	....	15
16	....	....	16

Exercise 5: Can you write them in Arabic?

N	Transliteration	Arabic	N
1	....	....	1
2	....	....	2
3	....	....	3
4	....	....	4
5	....	....	5
6	....	....	6
7	....	....	7
8	....	....	8
9	....	....	9
10	....	....	10
11	....	....	11
12	....	....	12
13	....	....	13
14	....	....	14
15	....	....	15
16	....	....	16

Exercise 6: Conjugate the below verbs in present tense

English	Transliteration	Arabic	Pro
I take	'a'akhuTh	أخُذ	أنا 'anaa
We take	na'akhuTh	نَأخُذ	نَحْن naHnu
You take (male)			أنْتَ 'anta
You take (female)			أنْتِ 'anti
You take (plural)			أنتم 'antum
He takes			هُوَ huwa
She takes			هِيَ heya
They take			هُمْ hum

English	Transliteration	Arabic	Pro
I try	'ujar-reb	أجَرّب	أنا 'anaa
We try	nujar-reb	نُجَرّب	نَحْن naHnu
You try (male)			أنْتَ 'anta
You try (female)			أنْتِ 'anti
You try (plural)			أنتم 'antum
He tries			هُوَ huwa
She tries			هِيَ heya
They try			هُمْ hum

English	Transliteration	Arabic	Pro
I think	'aTHun-n 'an-n	أظُنّ أنّ	أنا 'anaa
We think	naTHun-n 'an-n	نَظُنّ أنّ	نَحْن naHnu
You think (male)			أنْتَ 'anta
You think (female)			أنْتِ 'anti
You think (plural)			أنتم 'antum
He thinks			هُوَ huwa
She thinks			هِيَ heya
They think			هُمْ hum

Exercise 7: Write down a list of clothes you want to buy

1- ....   2- ....

3- ....   4- ....

5- ....   6- ....

7- ....   8- ....

9- ....   10- ....

Exercise 8: Fill in the blanks using the vocabulary you have learned, to make a dialogue.

Sara: Can I try this sweater on, please?

S: ....
..............................?

سارہ: ....
...............................؟

Clerk: Certainly. The fitting room is over there.

C: ....
....

المُوَظَّف: ....
....

Clerk: How is the size?

C: ....?

المُوَظَّف: ....؟

Sara: I think it's big, have you got a smaller size?

S: ....
..............................?

سارة: ....
....

Exercise 9: What does it mean?

....	*tasaw-wuq*	تَسَوُّق
....	*ulqii naTHra*	أَلقي نَظْرة
....	*khaSm*	خَصْم
....	*aw-walan*	أَوْلاً
....	*kul shay'*	كُلْ شَيْء
....	*bet-ta'kiid*	بالتَّأْكيد
....	*ghurfat al-qeyaas*	غُرْفَة القِياس
....	*almaqaas*	المَقاسْ
....	*mukhtalef /a*	مُخْتَلِف / ـة

Exercise 10: Can you find the 4 Arabic meanings for the words in the word square below?

1- different

2- everything

3- I think that

4- possible

5- first

ي	مُ	خ	ت	ل	ف	ر
ك	ل	ش	ي	ء	أَ	ز
ك	أ	ظّ	نّ	أ	نّ	ى
م	م	ك	ن	ا	ت	ف
ق	أ	و	ل	ا	ح	ـة

Vocabulary

shopping, تَسَوُّق
tasaw-wuq

I have a look, ألقي نَظْرة
ulqii naTHra

sale, خَصْم
khaSm

first, أوَّلاً
aw-walan

everything, كُلْ شَيْء
kul shay'

sweater, سُتْرة
sutra

dress, فُستان
fustaan

Shirt, قَميص
qamiiS

suit, بَدْلة
badlah

pants, بَنْطَلون
banTaluun

Scarf, طُرحة
TarHa

socks, جَوارب
jawaaareb

tie, ربْطة عُنُق
rabTat Aunuq

certainly, بالتَّأكيد
bet-ta'kiid

fitting room, غُرْفة القِياس
ghurfat al-qeyaas

large, واسِع / ة
waseA/a

tight, ضَيْق / ة
Day-yeq/a

size, المَقاس
almaqaas

different, مُخْتَلِف / ة
mukhtalef/a

colors, ألْوان
'alwaan

blue, أزْرَق

clothes, مَلابِس
malaabes

I think, أظُنّ
'aTHun

skirt, تَنّورة
tan-noura

hat, قُبَّعة
qub-baAa

high heel, كَعْب عالي
kaAb Aalii

belt, حِزام
Hezaam

shoe, حِذاء
HeThaa'

pink, زَهْري
zahryy

orange, بُرْتُقالي
burtuqaalyy

brown, بُنّي
bun-nyy

silver, فِضّي
feD-Dyy

golden, ذَهَبي
Thahabyy

red, أحْمَر
'aHmar

yellow, أصْفَر
'aSfar

green, أخْضَر
'akhDar

I wear, ألْبَس
'albas

I take off, أخْلَع
'akhlaA

I buy, أشْتَري
'ashtarii

I look, أنْظُر
'anTHur

I'd like, أوَدّ
'awad-d

I try, أجَرّب

'azraq
black, أَسْوَد
'aswad
white, أَبْيَض
'abyaD
'ujar-reb

UNIT ELEVEN

Looking for an Apartment

UNIT ELEVEN

Looking for an Apartment

Contents

- Looking for an Apartment

- Vocabulary

- Culture notes

- Grammar usage

  Asking about how much and how many

- Exercises

Looking for an Apartment

البَحْث عَنْ شَقّة

Al-baHth Aan shaq-qa

Dialogue

English	Transliteration	Arabic
Adam: Hello.	*A: as-salaamu Alaykum.*	آدم: السّلامُ عَلَيْكم.
The owner: Welcome.	*L: wa Aalaykum es-salaam.*	المالِك: وَعَلَيْكُم السّلام.
Adam: Excuse me; I'm calling to ask about your ad for the apartment for rent.	*A: law samaHt, 'anaa at-taSel le'as'al Aan eAlaankum Aan shaq-qa lil'eijaar!*	آدم: لو سَمَحْت؛ أنا أتّصِل لِأسْأل عَنْ إعلانكم عَنْ شَقّة للإيجار!
The owner: Yes, you are welcome.	*L: naAam tafaD-Dal*	المالِك: نَعَم تَفَضّل.
Adam: Could you give me more information, please?	*A: hal men al-mumken 'an 'aArif maAluumaat akthar men faDlek?*	آدم: هَلْ مِن المُمْكِن أنْ أعْرِف مَعْلومات أكْثَر مِنْ فَضلِك؟
The owner: Sure, what would you like to know?	*L: 'akiid; maThaa turiid 'an taAref?*	المالِك: أكيد؛ ماذا تُريد أنْ تَعْرِف؟
Adam: How many rooms does it have?	*A: kam ghurfa behaa?*	آدم: كَمْ غُرْفة بها؟
The owner: It has a reception room, a dining room, a small kitchen, two bedrooms and a large bathroom.	*L: behaa ghurfat esteqbaal,wa ghurfat sufra,wa maTbakh Saghiir,wa ghurfatayn len-nawm,wa Ham-maam kabiir.*	المالِك: بِها غُرْفَة اسْتِقْبال، وغُرْفَة سُفْرة؛ وَمطْبَخ صَغير، وَغُرْفَتين لِلنوم؛ وحَمّام كَبير.
Adam: How much is the rent?	*A: wa kam al-'eijaar?*	آدم: وَكَمْ الإيجَار؟
The owner: 700 USD per month.	*L: 700 sabAumaa'at dollar beash-shahr.*	المالِك: 700 سَبعمائة

دولار بالشّهر

Adam: That's too much!. Is it furnished?	*A: haThaa kathiir!. hal heya mafruusha?*	آدم:هَذا كَثير! هَل هِيَ مَفْروشَة؟
The owner: Yes, and it has its own parking.	*L: naAam walahaa mawqaf khaaS (Garage).*	المالِك: نَعَم. وَلَها مَوْقف خاص (جراج).
Adam: When can I see it?	*A: mataa yumken 'an 'araahaa?*	آدم: مَتَى يُمْكن أنْ أراها؟
The owner: You can come now. I'm in the office until the evening.	*L: yumkenuk 'an tajii' al'aan, fu'unua mawjuud bel-maklab elaa al-masaa'.*	المالِك: يُمكِنك أن تجيْء الآن؛ فأنا مَوجود بالمَكْتَب إلى المَساء.
Adam: I'll come to you within one hour, hopefully.	*A: sa'ajii' baAd saaAa in shaa' allah.*	آدم: سَأجيْء بَعْدَ ساعَة إنْ شاءَ الله .
The owner: You are welcome.	*L: 'ahlan wa sahlan.*	المالِك: أهْلاً وَسَهلاً

Vocabulary

English	Transliteration	Arabic
owner / landlord	*maalek*	مالِك
man maalek haThehe es-say-yaara		مَن مالك هذه السيارة؟
advertisement	*'eAlaan*	إعْلان
laa uHeb 'eAlaanat at-telefezion Aendama ushaahed filman		لا أحب إعلانات التلفزيون عندما أشاهد فيلما
apartment	*shaq-qa*	شَقّة

haThehe shaq-qa kabiira wa jamiila		هذه شقة كبيرة وجميلة
house / villa	*bayt*	بَيت
baytii Saghiir wa laken uHebhu		بيتي صغير؛ ولكن أحبه
hotel apartment	*shaq-qa funduqy-ya*	شَقّة فُنْدُقية
Aendamaa saafartu ilaa qatar, sakantu fii shaq-qa funduqy-ya		عندما سافرت إلى قطر؛ سكنت في شقة فندقية
I know	*'aAref*	أَعْرِف
information	*maAluumaat*	مَعْلومات
any	*'ayy*	أيّ
uHeb 'an 'aAref maAluumaat Aan 'ayy balad qabl as-safar ilayh		أحب أن أعرف معلومات عن أي بلد قبل السفر إليه
room / rooms	*ghurfa / ghuraf*	غُرفة / غُرَف
reception room	*ghurfat esteqbaal*	غُرْفَة استِقْبال
dining room	*ghurfat sufra*	غُرْفَة سُفْرة
kitchen /s	*maTbakh / maTaabekh*	مَطْبَخ / مَطابخ
sleeping room	*ghurfat an-nawm*	غُرْفَة النَّوم
bathroom /s	*Ham-maam / aat*	حَمّام / حمامات
Aendii shaq-qa kabiira, behaa ghurfat		عندي شقة كبيرة؛ بها غرفة

esteqbaal wa ghrfat sufra, wa maTbakh, wa 4 ghuraf nawm, wa 3 Ham-maamaat		استقبال؛ وغرفة سفرة؛ ومطبخ؛ و4 غرف نوم؛ و3 حمامات
parking /s	mawqaf / mawaaqef	مَوْقف / مواقف
'amshii ilaa maktabii kul yawm, lea'an almawqaf baAiid		أمشي إلى مكتبي كل يوم؛ لأن الموقف بعيد
when	mataa	مَتَى
God willing / hopefully	'en shaa' allah	إنْ شاءَ اللّه
mataa naThhab ila as-suuq? baAd saaAa 'en shaa' allah		متى نذهب إلى السوق؟ بعد ساعة إن شاء الله
private	khaaS	خاص
public	Aaam	عام
hal Aendak mawqaf khaaS les-say-yaara Aend al-bayt? laa, hunaak mawqaf Aaam		هل عندك موقف خاص للسيارة عند البيت؟ لا؛ هناك موقف عام
expensive	ghaalii	غالي
cheap	rakhiiS	رخيص
hal huwa ghaalii? laa, rakhiiS, bederham les-saaAa		هل هو غالي؟ لا رخيص؛ بدرهم للساعة
rent	eijaar	إيْجار
hal Aendakum shaq-qa lel-eijaar?		هل عندكم شقة للإيجار؟

Say it in Arabic

1- Can I speak to the owner of this house please?

2- There is an advertisment of a house for rent on the internet

3- I'd like to know more information about Arab countries

4- Do you have a reception / dining room in your apartment?

5- How many bedrooms does the apartment have?

6- How many bathrooms does it have?

7- Is there parking nearby?

8- When can I come to see the apartment?

9- I like the apartment but the rent is expensive

10- How much is the rent please?

Fill in the blanks with one of the new Vocabulary

1- shaq-qatii behaa 3 .... nawm.

1- شـقتي بها 3 .... نوم.

2- men almumken 'an .... maAluumaat Aan 'ayy balad Aaraby Aala al-internt.

2- من الممكن أن .... معلومات عن أي بلد عربي على الإنترنت.

3- hunaak .... Aan shaq-qa leleijaar Aala al-internet

3- هناك .... عن شقة للإيجار على الإنترنت.

4- ash-shaq-qa behaa .... esteqbaal, wa .... sufra.

4- الشـقة بها .... استقبال؛ و .... سـفرة.

5- haThaa albayt kabiir, wa lahu .... khaaS les-say-yaara.

5- هذا البيت كبير؛ وله .... خاص للسيارة.

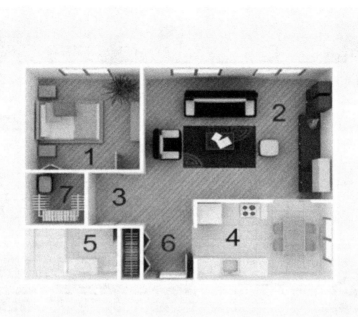

N	Transliteration	Arabic	N
1	*ghurfat nawm*	غُرْفة نوم	1
2	*ghurfat maAiisha*	غُرْفة مَعيشة	2
3	*rudha*	رُدْهَة	3
4	*maTbakh*	مَطْبَخ	4
5	*Ham-maam*	حَمّام	5
6	*mamar*	مَمَر	6
7	*ghurfat ghasiil*	غُرْفة غسيل	7

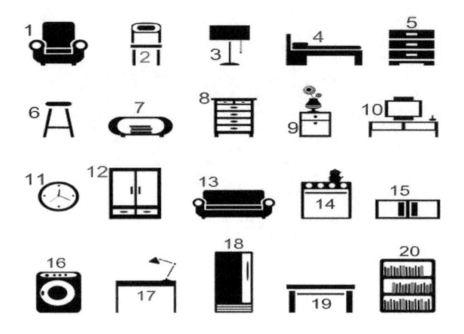

N	Transliteration	Arabic	N
1/2/6	kursyy	كُرسي	6/2/1
3	meSbaaH	مِصباح	3
4	sariir / feraash	سرير / فِراش	4
5/8	'adraaj	أدراج	8 / 5
6	kursyy	كُرسي	6
7	Taawelat shaay	طاوِلة شاي	7
9	khazanat sariir	خزانة سرير	9
10	telfezioun	تِلفزيون	10
11	saAa	ساعَة	11

12	khazaanat malaabes	خزانة ملابِس	12
13	Soufa	صوفة	13
14	mawqad /botaghaaz	مَوْقَد / بوتاغاز	14
15	khazaanat maTbakh	خَزانة مَطْبَخ	15
16	ghas-saala	غَسّالة	16
17	maktab	مَكْتَب	17
18	Thal-laaja "Fridge"	ثلاجة	18
19	sufra	سُفرة	19
20	maktaba	مَكْتَبة	20

Culture notes

The new society of Arabs still holds close to traditional values and morals. Loyalty to the family has always been and continues to be the top priority of the Arab. Religion is also a main focus in how Arabs live their lives.

One of the most important values in Arabic culture is generosity, which means a lot for Arabs. Even for poor people, as they love to give whatever they have, to be generous as much as possible and of course not everybody is the same, but that's one of the common general morals all over the Arab world.

Grammar usage

The most common way to ask (how many? How much?) is to use the interrogative particle "*kam*" كم

To ask about the numbers just use كم "*kam*" ? and use a singular noun after (*kam*). Marked with the suffix (*an*)(*tanween fat-ha*) **in formal Arabic.**

Example:

How many rooms are in the flat?	*Kam ghorfa fii ash-shaq-qa?*	كَمْ غُرْفَة في الشّقّة؟
How many days do you work in a week?	*Kam yawman taAmal fii al'usbuuA?*	كَمْ يَوْماً تَعمَل في الأسْبوع؟
How many books you have?	*Kam ketaban maAak?*	كم كتاباً مَعَك؟
How many kilos you want?	*Kam kiilou turiid?*	كم كيلو تُريد؟

The answer could be as:

ghurfa waaHeda / غُرفة واحدة one room

khamsat 'ay-yaam / خَمْسة أيّام five days

To ask about the price you can also use كَم "*Kam*"

How much is this shirt?	*Kam thaman/ seAr hathaa al-qamiiS?*	كم ثَمَن / سِعْر هذا القَمِيص ؟
What is the price of this shirt?		
How much is the rent?	*Kam al'iejaar?*	كم الإيجار؟
How much is per kilo?	*Kam thaman al-kiiluu?*	كم ثمن الكيلو؟

There's a simple way to ask about the price, just use the word (**bekam**?) بِكَم which mean = (how much?) for example:

How much is this shirt?	*beKam hathaa al-qamiiS?*	بكم هذا القميص ؟
How much is the kilo?	*bekam al-kiiluu?*	بكم الكيلو ؟
How much is the book?	*bekam al-ketaab?*	بكم الكتاب ؟

Note that the answer will be preceded by the preposition ـبِ "Be" if it`s number or currency , Examples

بجنيه *beguneih = 1 pound*	*bekam al-kiluu?*	بكم الكيلو ؟
بثلاثة جنيهات *bethalaath guneihaat =3 pounds*	*bekam al-ketaab?*	بكم الكتاب؟

Exercise 1: Translate into Arabic

1- How much is the coffee?

……………………………………………………………………

2- How many km is it from your work to your home?

……………………………………………………………………

3- How many days in a week?

……………………………………………………………………

4- How many months in a year?

……………………………………………………………………

5- How many weeks in a month?

……………………………………………………………………

6- How many hours in a day?

……………………………………………………………………

7- How many rooms in your house?

……………………………………………………………………

8- How many brothers do you have?

……………………………………………………………………

Exercise 2: Answer the above questions in Arabic after you translate them

1- ……………………………………………………………………

2- ……………………………………………………………………

3- ……………………………………………………………………

4- ……………………………………………………………………

5- ……………………………………………………………………

6- ……………………………………………………………………

7- ……………………………………………………………………

8- ……………………………………………………………………

Exercise 3: Can you write what you see in the picture in Arabic?

N	Transliteration	Arabic	N
1	………………………………	………………………………	1
2	………………………………	………………………………	2
3	………………………………	………………………………	3
4	………………………………	………………………………	4
5	………………………………	………………………………	5
6	………………………………	………………………………	6
7	………………………………	………………………………	7

Exercise 4: Can you write what you see in the picture in Arabic?

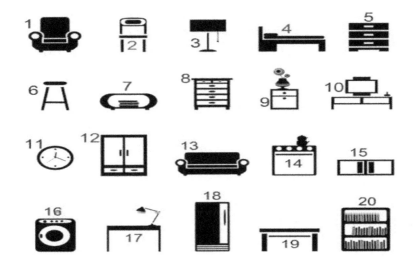

N	Transliteration	Arabic	N
3	....	....	3
4	....	....	4
5/8	....	....	8 / 5
6	....	....	6
7	....	....	7
9	....	....	9
10	....	....	10
11	....	....	11
12	....	....	12
13	....	....	13
14	....	....	14
15	....	....	15

Exercise 5: What does it mean?

....	Kam ghorfa fii ash-shaq-qa?	كَمْ غُرْفَة في الشّقّة؟
....	Kam yawman taAmal fii al'usbuuA?	كَمِ يَوْماً تَعمَل في الأسْبوع؟
....	Kam ketaban maAak?	كم كتاباً مَعَك؟
....	Kam kiilou turiid?	كم كيلو تُريد؟
....	Kam al'iejaar?	كم الإيجار؟
....	beKam hathaa al-qamiiS?	بكم هذا القميص ؟

Exercise 6: Build the dialogue

Adam: How much is the rent?	A:..........................?	آدم: ....؟
The owner: 700 USD per month.	L:.........................	المالِك: ....
Adam: That's too much!. Is it furnished?	A:........................ ....?	آدم:....................... .... ؟
The owner: Yes, and it has its own parking (Garage).	L:	المالِك: ....

Exercise 7: Match the words in **A** with the correct meanings in **B**

B		A	
The owner		ghurfat esteqbaal	غُرْفَة اسِتقْبال
advertisement		ghurfat sofra	غُرْفَة سُفْرة
apartment		maTbakh	مَطْبَخ
I know		ghurfat an-nawm	غُرْفَة النَّوم
information		Ham-maam	حَمّام
reception room		almaalek	المالِك
dining room		'eAlaan	إعْلان
kitchen		shaq-qa	شَقّة
sleeping room		'aAref	أعْرِف
bathroom		maAluumaat	مَعْلومات
parking		mawqaf	مَوْقف
when		mataa	مَتَى

Exercise 8: Conjugate the below verbs in present tense

English	Transliteration	Arabic	Pro
I see	*'ashuuf*	أشـوف	أنا `anaa
We see	*nashuuf*	نَـشـوف	نَحْن `naHnu
You see (male)			أنْتَ `anta
You see (female)			أنْتِ `anti
You see (plural)			أنتم `antum
He sees			هُوَ huwa
She sees			هِيَ heya
They see			هُمْ hum

English	Transliteration	Arabic	Pro
I come	*'ajii'*	أجـيء	أنا `anaa
We come	*najii'*	نَـجيء	نَحْن `naHnu
You come (male)			أنْتَ `anta
You come (female)			أنْتِ `anti
You come (plural)	*tajii'uun / tajii'uu*	تجيئون / تجيئوا	أنتم `antum
He comes			هُوَ huwa
She comes			هِيَ heya
They come			هُمْ hum

Exercise 9: Describe your own house/ apartment in a few lines. Mentioning how many rooms do you have?

....

....

....

....

....

Exercise 10: Can you find the 4 Arabic meanings for the words in the word square below?

1- advertisement

2- information

3- kitchen

4- apartment

5- toilet

ي	إ	ع	ل	ا	ن	ر
م	ع	ل	و	م	آ	ت
ك	ن	م	ط	ب	خ	ى
ع	ش	قّ	ة	ا	ت	ف
ق	ح	مّ	ا	م	ح	ة

Vocabulary

owner / landlord, مالِك
maalek

advertisement, إِعْلان
'eAlaan

apartment, شَقَّة
shaq-qa

house / villa, بَيت
bayt

hotel apartment, شَقَّة فُنْدُقية
shaq-qa funduqy-ya

I know, أعْرِف
'aAref

information, مَعْلومات
maAluumaat

reception room, غُرْفَة استِقْبال
ghurfat esteqbaal

dining room, غُرْفَة سُفرة
ghurfat sofra

kitchen, مَطْبَخ
maTbakh

sleeping room / bedroom, غُرْفَة النَوم
ghurfat an-nawm
ghurfat maAiisha

lounge, رُدْهَة
rudha

I see, أشوف
'ashuuf

I come, أجيء
'ajii'

bed, سرير / فِراش
sariir / feraash

tea table, طاوِلَة شاي
Taawelat shaay

closet, خزانة ملابِس
khazaanat malaabes

stove, مَوْقَد / بوتاغاز
mawqad /botaghaaz

washing machine, غَسّالة
ghas-saala

bathroom, حَمَّام
Ham-maam

parking, مَوْقف
mawqaf

when, مَتَى
mataa

God willing / hopefully, إِن شَاءَ الله
'en shaa' allah

private, خاص
khaaS

public, عام
Aam

expensive, غالي
ghaalii

cheap, رخيص
rakhiiS

pound, جنيه
guneih

dirhm, درهم
derham

living room, غُرْفة مَعيشة
fridge, ثلاجة
Thal-laaja

dinning table, سُفرة
sufra

sofa, صوفة
Soufa

bookshelves, مَكْتَبة
maktaba

Visit the book website to find out more!
http://www.LetsTalkArabic.com

UNIT TWELVE

Weekend Plan

UNIT TWELVE

Weekend Plan

Contents

- Dialogue: Weekend Plan

- Vocabulary

- Culture notes

- Grammar usage: Future tense

- Exercises

What's your weekend plan?

ما بَرْنامَجُكَ يَوْم العُطْلَة؟

maa barnaamajuka yawm al-AuTla?

Read the dialogue below as Adam has phoned Sara, asking her about her plan for the weekend.

English	Transliteration	Arabic
Adam: Hello Sara. Adam speaking.	*A: marHaban sara. 'anaa adam.*	آدَم: مَرْحَبا سارة. أنا آدم.
Sara: Hello Adam. How are you today?	*S: 'ahlan 'adam. kayfa Haaluka alyuwm?*	سارة: أهْلاً آدم. كَيْف حالُكَ اليوم؟
Adam: I'm fine. What will you do at the weekend? Do you have any plan yet?	*A: bekhayr, alHmdu lilah . maThaa sa-taAmaliin yawm al-AuTla? hal Aendake barnaamaj lahaa baAd?*	آدم: بِخَير؛ الحَمْدُ لله؛ ماذا ستَعْمَلين يَوْم العُطْلَة؟ هَلْ عِنْدكِ أي بَرْنامَج لَها بَعْد؟
Sarah : Not yet. Do you and our **colleagues** have any plan?	*S: 'elaa al'aan laa. hal Aendakum shay' 'anta wa z-zumalaa'?*	سارة: إلى الآن: لا؛ هَلْ عندكم شَيء أنتَ والزُّمَلاء؟
Adam: We'll go to the theatre on Friday evening, there's a show for Pygmalion play, then we'll go to have dinner? What is your opinion?	*A: sanaTh-hab lilmasraH yawm aljumAa fii elmasaa, hunaak AarD lemasraHeyat begmalion? wa baAdahaa naTh-hab lelAashaa'? maa ra'yuke?*	آدم: سنَذهَب لِلمَسْرح يَوم الجُمْعَة في المَساء؛ هُناك عَرْض لِمَسْرَحِيّة بغْماليون؟ وَبعْدَها سَوْفَ نَذْهَب لِلْعَشاء؟ما رَأيْكِ ؟
Sarah: I think it is a good idea.	*S: 'aTHun 'an-nahaa fekra jay-yeda.*	سارة: أظُنّ أنها فِكْرَة جَيّدَة.
Adam: Alright. We'll call you on Thursday evening to set the time/ hopefully "God willing".	*A: Hasanan. sawfa nat-taSel beke masaa' al-khamiis 'en shaa' Allah lenuHad-ded al-mawAed.*	آدم: حَسَناً؛ سَوْفَ نَتّصِل بكِ مَساء الخَميس إنْ شَاء الله؛ لَنُحَدّد المَوْعِد.
Sara: Thanks for your call Adam. Good-bye.	*S: shukran Alaa telefuunak ya 'adam. fii 'amaan ellah.*	سارة: شُكراً على تليفونك يا آدم؛ في أمان الله.
Adam: Good-bye.	*A: maAa as-salaama.*	آدم: مَعَ السّلامَة.

Vocabulary

English	Transliteration	Arabic
weekend / holiday	AuTla	عُطْلة
weekend / vacation	ijaaza	إجازة
uriid 'an 'akhuTh ijaaza shahr haThehe es-sana		أريد أن آخذ إجازة شهر هذه السنة
plan	khuT-Ta	خُطْة
laysa Aendii khuT-Ta lehaThehe lAuTla		ليس عندي خُطة لهذه العطلة
program	barnaamaj	بَرْنامَج
hunaak barnaamaj jay-yed fii t-telefzion al'aan		هناك برنامج جيد في التلفزيون الآن
opinion	ra'y	رَأْي
theatre	masraH	مسْرَح
maa ra'yukum 'an naThhab ilal-masraH haTha almasaa'		ما رأيكم أن نذهب إلى المسرح هذا المساء؟
cinema	siinemaa	سينما
opera	al-opera	الأوبرا
park / garden	Hadiiqa	حَديقة
Aendanaa Hadiiqa jamiila 'amaam albayt		عندنا حديقة جميلة أمام البيت
picnic	nuzha	نُزْهة
beach	shaaTe'	شاطِىء
uHeb 'an 'akhruj fii nuzha Aala ash-shaaTe' yawm al-jumuAa		أحب أن أخرج في نزهة على الشاطئ يوم الجمعة

play / show	Amal/ masraHy-ya	عَمل/مَسْرَحِية
hunaak masraHy-ya kumedy-ya fit-telefzion haTha al'masaa'		هناك مسرحية كوميدية في التلفزيون هذا المساء
he sets the time	yuHad-ded alwaqt	يُحدِد الوَقت
tomorrow	ghadan-bukrah	غَدَاً- بُكْرَة
nuriid 'an nuHad-ded al-waqt lenakhruj ghadan		نريد أن نحدد الوقت لنخرج غدا
later	fii maa baAd-laHeqan	فيما بَعْد- لاحِقاً
'anaa mashguul al'aan, natakal-lam fii maa baAd		أنا مشغول الآن؛ نتكلم فيما بعد

Say it in Arabic

1- What are you doing on the weekend?

2- Do you have a plan for this evening?

3- What's your program today?

4- What's your opinion of going to an Arabic restaurant for lunch?

5- There is a nice movie in the cinema this week

6- Do you have a garden at home?

7- Would you like to go for a picnic on the beach?

8- Can I set a time with you to talk about this?

9- See you tomorrow

10- See you later

Fill in the blanks with one of the new Vocabulary

1- maaThaa tafAal haThehe ....?

١- ماذا تفعل هذه ....؟

2- hal Aendak .... leyawm aljumuAa?

٢- هل عندك .... ليوم الجمعة؟

3- maa .... 'an naThhab ila almaTAam alhindi aljadiid?

٣- ما .... أن نذهب إلى المطعم الهندي الجديد؟

4- hunaak .... kabiira fii wasaT almadiina, naThhab ilaa hunaak kul yawm sabt.

٤- هناك .... كبيرة في وسط المدينة؛ نذهب إلى هناك كل يوم سبت.

5- uHeb 'an 'aThhab fii .... Aala ash-shaaTe' yawm as-sabt SabaaHan.

٥- أحب أن أذهب في .... على الشاطئ يوم السبت صباحا.

Culture Notes

It is very common in Arabic culture to say the phrase (*in shaa' Allah* إن شاء الله) when you talk about something that you are going to do in the future, and it is almost like when you say (hopefully) in English.

Grammar usage

The Future Tense.

Expressing the future tense in the Arabic language is very simple, as you can just add the prefix سَـ (*sa*) or the word سَوْفَ (*sawfa*) before the verb in present tense which means (will) You can use سَـ (*sa*) for the near future and سوف (*sawfa*) for the far future:

I will go to the beach tomorrow	سَـأَذْهَب إلى الشّاطِىء غَداً
	sa-'aThhab elaa ash-shaaTe' ghadan

Next Friday we will go to the cinema	سَوْف نَذْهَب للسّينِما الجُمُعَة القادِمَة
	sawfa naTh-hab les-siinemaa aljumuAa alqaadema

I will study Arabic next month

سَوْفَ أَدْرُس العَرَبِيّة الشّـهْر القادِم

sawfa 'adrus al-Aaraby-ya ash-shahr al-qaadem

Negating the future tense

For negating the future tense, you can use just the particle (*lan*) "لَن"=(will not) before the present tense. For example:

I will not travel on the vacation

لَن أسافِر في العُطْلَة

lan usaafer fii elAuTla

I will not eat sushi from now on

لَن آكُل سوشي بَعْد الآن

lan 'aakul suushii baAd al'aan

Exercise 1: Translate into Arabic

1- I have a vacation next month.

……………………………………………………..

2- I have a plan for my vacation.

……………………………………………………..

3- I want to go to the beach.

……………………………………………………..

4- I will go with my friend John.

……………………………………………………..

5- I will call him this evening to set the time.

……………………………………………………..

6- We'll go to the Cinema in the evening.

……………………………………………………..

7- But we are not going for dinner.

……………………………………………………..

8- Because we are going to eat at home.

……………………………………………………..

9- I think it is a good idea.

……………………………………………………..

10- I'm traveling next holiday.

……………………………………………………..

11- I will not eat showerma from now on.

……………………………………………………..

Exercise 2: Conjugate the verbs below in the future tense

English	Transliteration	Arabic	Pro
I'll call			أنا
We'll call			نَحْن
You'll call (male)			أنْتَ
You'll call (female)			أنْتِ
You'll call (plural)			أنتم
He'll call	sa-yat-taSel	سَيَّتَّصِل	هُوَ
She'll call			هِيَ
They'll call			هُمْ

English	Transliteration	Arabic	Pro
I'll be			أنا
We'll be			نَحْن
You'll be (male)			أنْتَ
You'll be (female)			أنْتِ
You'll be (plural)			أنتم
He'll be	sa-yakuun	سَيَكون	هُوَ
She'll be			هِيَ
They'll be			هُمْ

English	Transliteration	Arabic	Pro
I'll determine			أنا
We'll determine			نَحْن
You'll determine (male)			أنْتَ
You'll determine (female)			أنْتِ
You'll determine (plural)			أنتم
He'll determine	sa-yuHad-ded	سَيُحَدّد	هُوَ
She'll determine			هِيَ
They'll determine			هُمْ

English	Transliteration	Arabic	Pro
I'll go			أنا
We'll go			نَحْن
You'll go (male)			أنْتَ
You'll go (female)			أنْتِ
You'll go (plural)			أنتم
He'll go	sa-yaTh-hab	سَيَذهَب	هُوَ
She'll go			هِيَ
They'll go			هُمْ

English	Transliteration	Arabic	Pro
I'll see			أنا
We'll see			نَحْن
You'll see (male)			أنْتَ
You'll see (female)			أنْتِ
You'll see (plural)			أنتم
He'll see	sa-yashouf	سَيَشوف	هُوَ
She'll see			هِيَ
They'll see			هُمْ

English	Transliteration	Arabic	Pro
I'll come			أنا
We'll come			نَحْن
You'll come (male)			أنْتَ
You'll come (female)			أنْتِ
You'll come (plural)			أنتم
He'll come	sa-yajii'	سَيَجيء	هُوَ
She'll come			هِيَ
They'll come			هُمْ

Exercise 3: Fill in the blanks using the vocabulary you have learned, to make a dialogue

Adam: What do you have for the weekend?

A: ....

...........................?

آدم: ....

...................؟

Sarah: Not yet. Do you have any plans?

S: ....

...........................?

سارة: ....

....

....

Adam: We'll go to the theatre on Friday evening, Then we'll go to have dinner?
What is your opinion?

A: ....

....

...........................?

آدم: ....

....

...................؟

Sarah: I think it is a good idea.

S: ....

....

سارة: ....

....

Exercise 4: Match each word in **A** with an appropriate meaning in **B**

B		A
weekend	ijaaza	إجازة
plan	khuT-Ta	خُطّة
program	barnaamaj	بَرْنامَج
picnic	nuzha	نُزْهة
beach	shaaTe'	شاطِىء
he sets the time	yuHad-ded alwaqt	يُحِدِد الوَقت
later	fii maa baAd	فيما بَعْد

Exercise 5: Choose the correct answer:

1- 'adam .... fii madiina saghiira.　　　　١- آدم .... في مَدينة صَغَيَرة.

٣- أسكُن 'askun	٢- سَيسكُن sayaskun	١- تَسكُن taskun

2- hal .... Dajaaj ya Muhammad　　　　٢- هل............. دجاج يا مُحَمَّد.

٣- ستَأكُل sata'akul	٢- تَأكُلي ta'akulii	١- أكَلْ 'akal

3-'akhii .... Fii jaameAat 'abu dhadi.　　　　٣- أخي .... في جامعة أبوظبي

٣- سَيدرُس sayadrus	٢- أدرُس 'adrus	١- يَدْرُسـون yadrusuun

4- 'anaa .... AaSiir burtuqaal.　　　　٤- أنا .... عَصير بُرثُقال .

٣- يُريدوا turiiduu	٢- سأشرَب sa'shrab	١- شَرِبْ shareb

5- maaThaa .... yaa kariim.?　　　　٥- ماذا .... يا كريم ؟

٣- تَحبوا tuHebuu	٢- ستشرَب satashrab	١- يُحِب yuHeb

6- 'abii .... qahwa fii S-SabaaH.　　　　٦- أبي .... قَهْوَة في الصباح

٣- تَشْرَب tashrab	٢- سيشرب sayashrab	١- يَأكُل ya'kul

7-...... maAa 'ausratii fii bayt kabiir.　　　　٧- .... مع أسرتي في بيت كبير.

٣- سَكَن sakan	٢- يَسكُن yaskun	١- سأسكُن sa'askun

Exercise 6: Conjugate the verbs below in future tense, on outside worksheet

English	Transliteration	Arabic
I work	'aAmal	أعمل
I know	'aAref	أعرف
I understand	'afham	أفهَم
I hear	'asmaA	أسـمَع
I read	'aqraa'	أقرَأ
I sit	'ajles	أجلِس
I enter	'adkhul	أدخُل
I go out	'akhruj	أخرُج
I watch	ushaahed	أشـاهِد
I travel	usaafer	أسـافِر

Exercise 7: Write down 5 sentences in Arabic about your weekend plan:

.... 1-

.... 2-

.... 3-

.... 4-

.... 5-

Exercise 8: Translate into English

1- Suzan satadkhul haThehe el-jaameAa.

١- سوزان سَتدخُل هذِهِ الجامِعَة.

....

....

2- ukhtii saara satakuun fii el-bayt.

٢- أخْتي سارَة سَتكون في البيت.

....

....

3- sa'akuun fii el-maktab.

٣- سأكون في المَكْتَب.

....

....

4- heya kaanat Taaleba fii el-kul-ly-ya.

٤- هِيَ كانت طالبَة في الكلّية.

....

....

5- kaana John yadrus al-Aaraby-ya.

٥- كان جون يَدرُس العَرَبِيّة.

....

....

Exercise 9: Can you find the four Arabic meanings for the words in the word square below?

1- vacation

2- program

3- opinion

4- plan

5- picnic

ي	إ	ج	ا	ز	ة	ر
أ	ب	ر	ن	ا	م	ج
ك	ر	أ	ي	ر	آ	ا
ت	أ	خ	طّ	ة	ر	ف
ق	ن	ز	ه	ة	ن	و

Exercise 10: Using the words below, fill in the puzzle with the meanings.

Down **Across**

1- today   2- before

3- after   4- tomorrow

5- yesterday

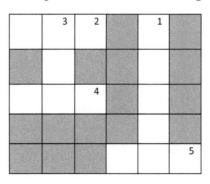

VOCABULARY

weekend / holiday, عُطْلة
Autla

weekend / vacation, إجازة
ijaaza

plan, خُطّة
khuT-Ta

program, بَرْنامَج
barnaamaj

opinion, رَأْي
ra'y

theatre, مسْرَح
masraH

cinema, سينما
siinemaa

park / garden, حَديقة
Hadiiqa

picnic, نُزْهة
nozha

beach, شاطِىء
shaaTe'

play / show, مَسْرَحِية
masraHy-ya

he sets the time, يُحدِد الوَقت
yuHad-ded alwaqt

tomorrow, غَدًا- بُكْرة
ghadan-bukrah

later, فيما بَعْد- لا حِقًا
fii maa baAd-laHeqan

He'll call, سَيَّتَصِل
sa-yat-taSel

He'll be, سَيَكون
sa-yakuun

He'll determine, سَيُحَدّد
sa-yuHad-ded

alright, حَسَنًا
hasanan

Adam Yacoub

UNIT THIRTEEN

Making an Appointment

UNIT THIRTEEN

Making an Appointment

Contents

- Making an Apointment

- Vocabulary

- Culture notes

- Grammar usage
  Negation of the nominal sentence

- Exercises

Adam Yacoub

Making an Appointment

Ta-Hdiid mawAed

تَحْديد مَوْعِد

English	Transliteration	Arabic
Receptionist: Hello, Dr. Khaled's Clinic here.	M: 'ahlan wasahlan, hunaa Aeyaadat ad-duktuur Khaled.	المُوَظّفَ: أهْلاً وَسَهْلاً؛ هُنا عِيادة الدّكْتور خَالِد.
Adam: Hello, this is Adam. I want to make an appointment with Dr. Khaled.	A: 'ahlan, 'anaa 'adam, uriid 'an uHad-ded mawAed maAa duktuur Khalid.	آدَم: أهْلا؛ أنا آدَم؛ أريد أنْ أحَدِّد مَوْعِد مَعَ دُكتور/ خَالِد.
Receptionist: May I know the reason for the consulting?	M: hal men al-mumken 'an 'aAref sabab alesteshaara?	المُوَظّفَ: هَلْ مِن المُمْكِن أن أعْرِف سَبَب الاسْتِشارَة؟
Adam: I have a sore throat.	A: Aendii eltehaab fii l-Halq.	آدَم: عِنْدي إلتِهاب في الحَلق.
Receptionist: Since when?	M: munThu mataa?	المُوَظّف: مُنْذ مَتَى؟
Adam: About three days.	A: munThu thalaathat 'ay-yaam.	آدم: مُنذ ثَلاثَة أيّام.
Receptionist: Is it suitable for you at 11:00 am tomorrow?	M: hal yunaasebuka ghadan. as-saaAa 11:00 SabaaHan?	المُوَظّف: هَلْ يُناسبك غدا. الساعة11:00 ص؟
Adam: Unfortunately, I don`t have time, what about 11:30 am?	A: lel'asaf,laysa Aendii waqt,maThaa Aan 11:30 SabaaHan?	آدم: للأسف ليس عندي وقت ,ماذا عن 11:30ص؟
Receptionist: Is 11:30 am good?	M: mumken as-saAa 11:30 SabaaHan hal haThaa jay-yed?	الموظف: مُمْكِن السّاعَة 11:30 صَباحاً؛ هَلْ هَذا جَيّد؟
Adam: Yes. That's good.	A: naAam, haThaa jay-yed.	آدم: نَعَم؛ هَذا جَيّد.
Receptionist: Okay, see you tomorrow hopefully.	M: Hasanan, naraaka ghadan 'en shaa' allah.	المُوَظّفَ: حَسَناً؛ نَراك غَداً إنْ شاء الله.
Adam: Thank you, bye.	A: shukran; maAa s-salaama.	آدم: شُكْراً؛ مَعَ السّلامَة.

Vocabulary

English	Transliteration	Arabic
receptionist	*mwaTH-THaf esteqbaal*	مُوَظّف اسْتِقْبال
Sadiiqatii mwaTH-THafat esteqbaal fil-maTaar		صديقتي موظفة استقبال في المطار
clinic	*Aeyaadah*	عِيادة
hospital	*mustashfaa*	مُستَشْفى
zawjatii Tabiiba, wa heya taAmal fii mustashfaa		زوجتي طبيبة؛ وهي تعمل في
SabaHan, wa fii Aeyaadah masaa'an		مستشفى صباحا؛ وفي عيادة مساء
meeting	*ejtemaaA*	إِجْتِماع
appointment	*mawAed*	مَوْعِد
nasaytu mawAed al-ejtemaaA alyawm.		نسيت موعد الاجتماع اليوم.
reason	*sabab*	سَبَب
since / ago	*munThu*	مُنْذُ
Sadiiqatii fil maktab laa tatakal-lam maAii		صديقتي في المكتب لا تتكلم معي
munThu 'ay-yaam, wa laa 'aAref as-sabab.		مُنذ أيام؛ ولا أعرف السبب.
suitable	*munaaseb*	مُنَاسِب
'aThun 'an al-waqt munaaseb le natakal-lam		أظن أن الوقت مناسب لنتكلم عن
Aan barnaamaj al-AuTla		برنامج العطلة
to suit	*yunaaseb*	يُناسِب
we meet	*nataqaabal*	نتقابل
hal yunaasebak 'an nataqaabal haaTha almasaa'		هل يناسبك أن نتقابل هذا المساء
as-saaAa 7?		الساعة 7؟

247

consulting	'esteshaara	اِسْتِشارَة
sore throat	eltehaab Halq	إلتِهاب حَلْق
uriid esteshaarat aT-Tabiib men faDlek, le'an Aendii eltehaab fil Halq		أريد اِستشارة الطبيب من فضلك؛ لأن عندي اِلتِهاب في الحلق!
interview	muqaabala	مُقابلة
Aendii muqaabala baAd aTH-THuhr		عندي مقابلة بعد الظهر
unfortunately	lel'asaf	للأسَف
okay	Hasanan	حَسَناً
hal 'anta mashghuul? naAam lel'asaf. Hasanan, naThhab ghadan		هل أنت مشغول؟ نعم للأسف. حسنا نذهب غدا
to determine / set a time	uHad-ded	أُحَدّد
sick	mariiD / a	مَريض / ـة
Sadiiqii mariiD munThu yawmain		صديقي مريض منذ يومين
I need	'aHtaaj	أحتاج
to see	'araa	أَرَى
'aHtaaj 'an 'araa aT-Tabiib		أحتاج أن أرى الطبيب لاحقا
not / don't	laysa	ليس
laysa Aendii waqt		ليس عندي وقت

Say it in Arabic

1- I have a friend who works as a receptionist in a clinic

2- Is there a hospital or a clinic nearby please?

3- I'd like to set an appointment with my manager for a meeting

4- What time is suitable for you to meet tonight?

5- I have a sore throat, I want to go for consulting the doctor

6- I need to see the doctor

7- I have no time, unfortunately

8- I'm so hungry! I haven't eaten anything since morning

Fill in the blanks with one of the new Vocabulary

1- *ukhtii Tabiiba fii* .... *al-qaahera*

١- أختي طبيبة في .... القاهرة.

2- *Aendii* .... *maAa al-mudiir baAd aTHuhr.*

٢- عندي .... مع المدير بعد الظّهر.

3- *hal* .... *'an nataqaabal haTha al-masaa'?*

٣- هل .... أن نتقابل هذا المساء؟

4- *lii Sadiiq fi elmaktab laa yatakal-lam*

maAii........... *'ay-yaam, beduun* ....

٤- لي صديق في المكتب لا يتكلم معي
.... أيام ؛ بدون .... !

5- .... *Aendii waqt haTha alusbuuA, 'anaa*

mashghuul jed-dan

٥- .... عندي وقت هذا الأسبوع؛ أنا
مشغول جدا.

Culture notes

There is a verb in Arabic which means (I can) = ('astaTiiA أستطيع). But it's very common in the Arab world to use the word (*mumken* مُمْكِن) which means (possible) instead of saying (can I / may I / is it possible?).

Grammar usage
Negation of the nominal sentence

We have learned the nominal sentence(the sentence which starts with a noun) in previous units. To negate the nominal sentence, you can use the word (*laysa* = لَيْسَ) which is conjugated as how the verbs in past tense look. Also it's considered an uncompleted verb in Arabic. For example:

English	Transliteration	Arabic
I am not sure about the working schedule.	*Lastu mota'akeddan men jadwal mawaaAiid al-Aamal*	لستُ متأكداً من جَدْول مَواعيد العَمَل.
The doctor is not in the clinic right now.	*Ad-duktur laysa fii al-Aeyaadah,al'an*	الدُكْتور لَيْسَ في العِيادَة الأن.
I don`t have time	*Laysa Aendii waqt.*	لَيْسَ عِنْدي وَقْت.

The following chart shows" *laysa*" conjugated with all the subject pronouns as the past tense conjugation:

English	Transliteration	Arabic	Subject
I am not	*lastu*	لَسْتُ	أنا
We are not	*lasnaa*	لَسْنا	نحن
You(m) are not	*lasta*	لَسْتَ	أنتَ
You(f) are not	*lasti*	لَسْتِ	أنتِ
You(p)are not	*lastum*	لَسْتم	أنتم
He is not	*laysa*	لَيْسَ	هو
She is not	*laysat*	لَيْسَت	هي
They are not	*laysuu*	لَيْسوا	هم

Examples:

English	Transliteration	Arabic
I am not an engineer	*lastu mohandesa*	لَسْتُ مُهَنْدِسَة
We are not students	*lasnaa Taalebaat*	لَسْنا طُالبات
She is not a teacher	*laysat mudar-resa*	لَيْسَتْ مُدَرّسَة
Eiffel tower is not in Germany	*burj 'eiifel laysa fii 'almaanyaa*	بُرْج ايفِل لَيْس في ألمانيا

Exercise 1: Translate into Arabic

1. May I make an appointment with the doctor please?

....

2. Is it possible to come tomorrow at 09:00 am?

....

3. Is it suitable for you to come in the evening?

....

4. I have sore throat for two days.

....

5. May I know the reason for the appointment?

....

Exercise 2: Translate into English

1. *Ahmad yaAmal muwaTH-THaf esteqbaal*

....

١. أحمد يعمل مُوَظّف اِسْتِقْبال

....

2. *munTHu mataa taskun hunaa?*

....

٢. مُنْذ مَتَى تَسكُن هُنا؟

....

3. *uriid 'an uHad-ded mawAed maAa al-mudiir.*

....

٣. أُريد أَنْ أُحَدِّد مَوْعِد مَع المُدير.

....

4. *'ana taAbaan munThu thalaathat 'ay-yaam.*

....

٤. أَنا تَعْبان مُنذ ثَلاثَة أَيّام.

....

5. *maa sabab alesteshara?*

....

٥. ما سَبَب الاسْتِشارَة ؟

....

Exercise 3: Choose the right form of ليس (laysa):

1- سارة .... لَها أُخت .

(لَسْتَ - لَيْسَتْ - ليسوا)

Sara .... lahaa ukht.

lasta – laysat – laysuu

2- أنا .... مِصْريّة ,أنا أَمْريكِيّة .

(لَسْنا- لَيْسَتْ- لَسْتُ)

'anaa ....meSry-ya, 'anaa amriiky-ya.

lasnaa – laysat - lastu

3- .... عندي وَقْت.

(لَيْسَ- لَسْتُ- لَسْتُم)

.............Aendii waqt.

laysa – lastu - lastum

4-آدم وسـارة .... مِنْ أَمْريكا

(لَيْسوا- لَسْتِ –لستم)

'adam wa sara .... men 'amriika.

laysuu – lasti - lastum

5- كَريم .... مَعَه سيّارة.

(لستم- ليس- لسنا)

Kariim .... maAahu say-yaara.

lastum – laysa - lasnaa

Exercise 4: Conjugate the verb below in the present tense

English	Transliteration	Arabic	Pro
I see	'araa	أرَى	أنا
We see			نَحْن
You see (male)			أنْتَ
You see (female)			أنْتِ
You see (plural)			أنتم
He sees	yaraa	يَرَى	هُوَ
She sees			هِيَ
They see			هُمْ

English	Transliteration	Arabic	Pro
I determine	'auHad-ded	أُحَدّد	أنا
We determine			نَحْن
You determine (male)			أَنْتَ
You determine (female)			أَنْتِ
You determine (plural)			أنتم
He determines	yuHad-ded	يُحَدّد	هُوَ
She determines			هِيَ
They determine			هُمْ

Exercise 5: Fill in the blanks using the vocabulary you have learned to make a dialogue

Receptionist: Is it suitable for you at 11:00 am tomorrow?

M: ....
...............................?

المُوَظّف: ....
...............................؟

Adam: Unfortunately, I don't have time, what about 11:30 am?

A: ....
...............................?

آدم : ....
.... ؟

Receptionist: Is 11:30 am good?

M: ....
...............................?

الموظف: ....
.... ؟

Adam: Yes. That's good.

A: naAam, haTHaa jay-yed.

آدم: نَعَم؛ هَذا جَيّد.

Receptionist: Okay, see you tomorrow hopefully.

M: ....
....

المُوَظّف: ....
....

253

Exercise 6: Match each word in (**A**) with the appropriate meaning in (**B**)

B		A	
clinic	Hasanan	حَسَناً
appointment	munThu	مُنْذُ
reason	uHad-ded	أَحَدّد
suitable	'araa	أرَى
consulting	laysa	لَيْسَ
unfortunately	lel'asaf	للأسَف
okay	Aeyaadah	عِيادة
since	mawAed	مَوْعِد
to determine / set a time	sabab	سَبَبْ
to see	munaaseb	مُنَاسِب
not	'esteshaara	اِسْتِشارَة

Exercise 7: Fill in the blanks with appropriate words

1. Ahmad yaAmal ———— esteqbaal.

١. أحمد يعمل ———— اِسْتِقْبال.

2. ———— mataa taskun hunaa?

٢. ——— مَتَى تَسكُن هُنا؟

3. uriid 'an ——— mawAed maAa al-mudiir.

٣. أُرِيد أَنْ ——— مَوْعِد مَع المُدِير.

4. 'ana taAbaan ——— thalaathat 'ay-yaam.

٤. أَنا تَعْبان ——— ثَلاَثَة أَيّام.

5. maa —— alesteshara?

٥. ما ——— الاسْتِشارَة ؟

Exercise 8: Choose the correct Arabic meanings for the English words words

A- Appointment

3- مَوْعِد	2- سَبَب	1- مُنَاسِب
mawAed	sabab	munaaseb

B- Suitable

3- مَوْعِد	2- سَبَب	1- مُنَاسِب
mawAed	sabab	munaaseb

C- Reason

3- مُنَاسِب	2- سَبَب	1- مَوْعِد
munaaseb	sabab	mawAed

D- Unfortunately

3- للأسَف	2- حَسَناً	1- مُنْذُ
lel'asaf	Hasanan	munThu

E- Okay

3- للأسَف	2- حَسَناً	1- مُنْذُ
lel'asaf	Hasanan	munThu

F- Since

3- للأسَف	2- حَسَناً	1- مُنْذُ
lel'asaf	Hasanan	munThu

G- To determine

3- لَيْسَ	2- أَحّدّد	1- أَرَى
laysa	uHad-ded	'araa

Exercise 9: Write an email in Arabic to your manager asking him or her to set up an appointment for meeting.

....

....

....

....

....

....

Exercise 10: Using the words below, fill in the puzzle with the meanings. Remember to go from right to left or up to down.

Down

1- to determine

2- hospital

3- clinic

Across

1- meeting

4- since

		4		3		2		1

VOCABULARY

receptionist, مُوَظَّف اسْتِقْبال

mwaTH-THaf esteqbaal

clinic, عِيادة

Aeyaadah

hospital, مُسْتَشْفى

mustashfaa

meeting, اِجْتِماع

ejtemaaA

appointment, مَوْعِد

mawAed

reason, سَبَبٌ

sabab

suitable, مُنَاسِب

munaaseb

to suit, يُنَاسِب

yunaaseb

consulting, اِسْتِشارَة

'esteshaara

sore throat, اِلْتِهاب حَلْق

eltehaab Halq

unfortunately, لِلأَسَف

lel'asaf

okay, حَسَنًا

Hasanan

since / ago, مُنْذُ

munThu

to determine / set a time, أُحَدّد

uHad-ded

to see, أَرَى

'araa

not, لَيْسَ

laysa

interview, مقابلة

muqaabala

to meet, تقابل

taqaabal

I need, أحتاج

aHtaaj

sick, مريض

mariiD

UNIT FOURTEEN

At the Clinic

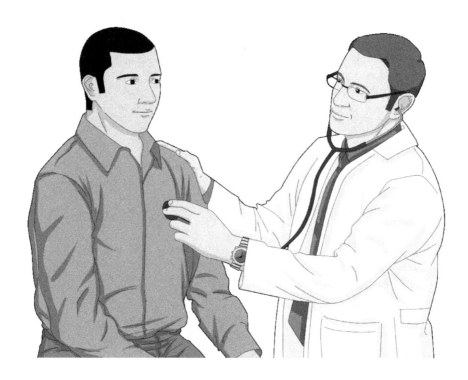

UNIT FOURTEEN

At the Clinic

Contents

- At the Clinic

- Vocabulary

- Culture notes

- Grammar usage
    Find more about (broken plural)

- Exercises

At the Clinic
fii l-Aeyaadah
فِي العِيادة

English	Transliteration	Arabic
Dr. Khaled: Good morning Adam. How do you feel?	D: SabaaH el-khayr ya 'adam, kayf tashAur?	د. خالِد: صَباح الخَير يا آدَم؛ كَيْف تَشْعُر؟
Adam: I have a bad sore throat.	A: Aendii eltehaab shadiid fii l-Halq!	آدَم: عِنْدي إلتِهاب شَديد في الحَلَق!
Dr. Khaled: When did it start?	D: munThu mataa bada'?	د. خالِد: مُنْذ مَتى بَدَأ؟
Adam: Three days ago.	A: munThu thalaathat 'ay-yaam.	آدَم: مُنذ ثَلاثَة أيّام.
Dr. Khaled: Do you have any other symptoms?	D: Hal Aendak 'ayy 'aAraaD ukhraa?	د. خالِد: هَلْ عِنْدَك أيّ أعْراض أُخْرَى؟
Adam: I have a slight fever.	A: 'ashAur beHum-maa Tafiifa.	آدَم: أشْعُر بحُمَّى طَفيفَة.
Dr. Khaled: Okay. I want to have a look at your throat.	D: Tay-yeb ureed 'an ulqii naTHra Aalaa Halqek.	د. خالِد: طَيّب؛ أريد أن أُلْقي نَظْرَة عَلَى حَلْقك.
Adam: Yes please.	A: tafaD-Dal.	آدَم: تَفَضّل.
Dr. Khaled: I'm going to write you a prescription for an antibiotic.	D: sa'aktub lak waSfat muDaad Hayawii.	د. خالِد: سَأكْتُب لَك وَصْفَة مُضاد حَيَوي.
Adam: How many times do I have to take this?	A: wakam mar-ra men l-laazem 'an 'akhuTh haThaa alAelaaj?	آدَم: وَكَمْ مَرّة مِن اللازم أنْ آخُذ هّذا العِلاج؟

Dr. Khaled: Take a pill three times a day for seven days. You'll probably feel better in a couple of days hopefully.	**D:** qurS; thalaath mar-raat fii alyawm, lemud-dat 'asbuuA. sawfa tashAur betaHas-sun khelal yawmayn 'en shaa' allah.	**د. خالد:** قُرص؛ ثَلاث مَرّات في اليَوم؛ لمُدّة أسْبوع؛ سَوْف تَشْعُر بتَحسّن خِلال يَوْمَين إن شَاءَ الله.
Adam: Thanks a lot, Dr. Khaled.	**A:** shukran jaziilan ya doktor khaled.	**آدم:** شُكْراً جَزيلا يا دُكتور خالِد.

Vocabulary

English	Transliteration	Arabic
I feel	'ashAur	أشْعُر
getting better	taHas-sun	تَحَسّن
antibiotic	muDaadd Hayawii	مُضادّ حَيَويّ
kuntu mariiD ams, wa laken 'akhaThtu muDaadd Hayawii wal-Hamdu lillah 'ashAur be-taHas-sun		كُنتُ مَريض أمْس؛ ولَكِن أخَذْتُ مُضاد حَيَويّ والحَمْدُ لله أشْعُر بِتَحسُّن الآن
to get better	yataHas-san	يَتَحَسّن
kayf adam? huwa yataHas-san, alhamdu lillah		كيف آدم؟ هو يتحسن؛ الحمد لله
light	khafiif / a	خَفيف/ ـة
heavy	Thaqiil/a	ثقيل / ـة
uHeb al-ghada' aTh-Thaqiil, wal-Aasha' alkhafiif		أحب الغداء الثقيل؛ والعشاء الخفيف
fever	Hum-maa	حُمّى
Sadiiqii mariiD be-Hum-maa munThu yawmain		صديقي مريض بحمى منذ يومين
cure	Aelaaj	عِلاج

medicine	dawaa'	دَواء
pill / tablet	qurS	قُرص
once	mar-ra	مَرّة
times	mar-raat	مَرّات
'akhuTh qurSan 3 mar-raat fil yawm men ad-dawaa'		آخُذ قرصا 3 مرات في اليوم من الدواء
symptoms	'aAraaD	أَعْراض
strong	shadiid/a	شَديد / ة
slight	Tafiif/a	طَفيف / ـة
It's necessary to	men al-laazem 'an	مِن اللازِم أن
yabduu Aalayk 'aAraaD Hum-maa Tafiifa! men al-laazem 'an taThhab le-Tabiib		يبدو عليك أعراض حمى طفيفة! من اللازم أن تذهب لطبيب
for a period	le-mud-da	لِمُدّة
Aamatu fii qaTar le-mud-dat sana		عملت في قطر لمدة سنة
during	khelaal	خِلال
men al-laazem 'an usaafer khelaal yawmain		من اللازم أن أسافر خلال يومين
prescription	waSfa	وَصْفَة
laa yumken 'an 'ashtarii ad-dawaa' beduun waSfa		لا يمكن أن أشتري الدواء بدون وصفة
other / another	ukhraa	أُخْرَى
mar-ra ukhraa men faDlek		مرة أخرى من فضلك
pain	'alam	أَلَمْ

Say it in Arabic

1- How do you feel today?

2- Did you take antibiotic?

3- I'd like to wear light clothes today

4- I had a fever last week

5- You have to (It's necessary to) take the cure to get better

6- I'm taking a pill 3 times a day

7- I need a prescription to buy the pills

8- You look sick

9- Did you take the medicine?

Fill in the blanks with one of the new Vocabulary

1- .... be-'alam fii Halqii.

1- .... بألم في حلقي.

2- laa uHeb al-Aasha' ...., laken khafiif

2- لا أحب أن آكل عشاء ....؛ لكن خفيف

3- kaanat Sadiiqatii mariiDa, wa laken al-yawm .... alHamdu lillah

3- كانت صديقتي مريضة؛ ولكنها اليوم .... الحمد لله.

4- 'adrus al-Aarabyya fiS-Saf 3 .... fil-'asbuuA

4- أدرس العربية في الصف 3 .... في الأسبوع.

5- mar-ra .... men faDlek!

5- مرّة .... من فضلك!

Parts of the Body

English	Transliteration	Arabic
head	raa's	رَأس
face	wajh	وَجْه
eye (Eyes)	Ain (Ainaan)	عَيْن (عَيْنان)
nose	'anf	أنْف
ear (Ears)	uThun (uThunaan)	أذن (أُذُنان)
mouth	fam	فَم
cheek (Cheeks)	khad (khuduud)	خَد (خُدود)
chin	Thaqn	ذَقْن
hair	shaAr	شَعْر
neck	raqaba	رَقَبَة
tooth (Teeth)	sen ('asnaan)	سِن (أسْنان)
shoulder (Shoulders)	katef ('aktaaf)	كَتِف (أكْتاف)
arm (Arms)	TheraaA(TheraaAaan)	ذِرَاع (ذِراعان)
hand (Hands)	yad (yadaan)	يَد (يدان)
finger (Fingers)	'eSbaA ('aSaabeA)	إَصْبِع (أصابِع)
chest	Sadr	صَدْر
elbow	kuuA	كوع

heart	qalb	قَلْب
belly	baTn	بَطْن
stomach	maAeda	مَعِدَة
leg (Legs)	rejl (arjul)	رِجْل (أَرْجُل)
knee (Knees)	rukba (rukbatain)	رُكْبَة (رُكبَتَين)
foot (Feet)	qadam (aqdaam)	قَدَم (أَقْدام)
back	THahr	ظَهْر

Culture Note
Useful Verbs

Practice learning & conjugating the new verbs below. As its considered *classical or old Arabic*, however most of them are commonly used in spoken Arabic.

يَشوف *yashuuf*
To look at

English	Transliteration	Arabic	Pro
I look at	'ashuuf	أشوف	أنا
We look at	nashuuf	نَشوف	نَحْن
You look at (male)	tashuuf	تَشوف	أنْتَ
You look at (female)	tashuufii / tashuufiin	تَشوفي / تَشوفين	أنْتِ
You look at (plural)	tashuufuu / tashuufuun	تَشوفوا / تَشوفون	أنتم
He looks at	yashuuf	يَشوف	هُوَ
She looks at	tashuuf	تَشوف	هِيَ
They look at	tashuufuu / yashuufuun	يَشوفوا / يَشوفون	هُمْ

Example:

هَلْ مِن المُمْكِن أَن أَشوف الشّقّة قَبْل الإيجار؟

hal men al-mumken 'an 'ashuuf ash-shaq-qa qabl al-'eiijaar?

Can I see the apartment before rent?

يَروح yaruuH
To go

English	Transliteration	Arabic	Pro
I go	*'aruuH*	أروح	أنا
We go	*naruuH*	نَروح	نَحْن
You go (male)	*taruuH*	تَروح	أنْت
You go (female)	*taruuHii / taruuHiin*	تَروحي / تروحين	أنْتِ
You go (plural)	*taruuHuu / taruuHuun*	تروحوا / تروحون	أنتم
He goes	*yaruuH*	يَروح	هُوَ
She goes	*taruuH*	تَروح	هِيَ
They go	*yaruuHuu / yaruuHuun*	يروحوا / يروحون	هُمْ

Grammar Usage

Broken plural

Few Arabic nouns cannot form the plural using the (feminine or masculine plural) which we have learned so far. Here we have some more patterns for the broken plural as we said before, that we will keep learning them one by one or two by two as we go.

The next chart shows some of the words in the singular form then with the broken plural form, so you can observe the changes.

English	Transliteration	Arabic
head (heads)	*raa's (ru'auus)*	رَأس (رُءوس)
eye (eyes)	*Ain (Auyuun)*	عَيْن (عُيُون)
nose (noses)	*'anf ('anuuf)*	أنْف (أنـوف)
cheek (cheeks)	*khad (khuduud)*	خَد (خُـدود)
chin (chins)	*Thaqn (Thuquun)*	ذَقْن (ذُقُون)
heart (hearts)	*qalb (quluub)*	قَلْب (قُلـوب)
belly (bellies)	*baTn (buTuun)*	بَطْن (بُطُون)
chest (chests / breasts)	*Sadr (Suduur)*	صَدْر (صُدُور)

Another pattern		
tooth (teeth)	sen ('asnaan)	سِين (أَسْنـان)
shoulder (shoulders)	katef ('aktaaf)	كَتِف (أَكْتـاف)
hand (hands)	yad ('ayaad)	يَد (أَيـاد)
finger (fingers)	'eSbaA ('aSaabeA)	إَصْيِع (أصـايِع)
foot (feet)	qadam ('aqdaam)	قَدَم (أَقْدام)
elbow (elbows)	kuuA ('akwaaA)	كوع (أَكْواع)

Exercise 1: Translate into Arabic:

1. I have a slight fever. I have to go to the doctor tomorrow.
....
2. I'm taking a pill three times a day for seven days, hopefully I will be better.
....
3. I don't know how many times I have to take this tablet!
....
4. I feel that I'm having fever symptoms.
....
5. I feel pain in my head. I have to take an aspirin tablet.
....
6. I feel pain in my stomach and my back.
....
7. It is necessary to take the medicine.
....
8. I feel better after taking the medicine.
....
9. How do you feel today?
....
10. Where is the hospital please?
....
11. Where is the clinic please?
....
12. I have to call the doctor.
....

Exercise 2: Translate into English

1- men al-laazem 'an aruuH le-doctuur.

.مِن اللازِم أن أروح لِدكتور .1

....

....

2- 'ayna Aeyaadat al'snaan men faDlek?

2- أين عِيادة الأسنان مِن فَضْلِك؟

....

....

3- kam mar-ra men al-laazem 'an 'akhuth alAelaaj?

3- كَمْ مَرّة مِنْ اللازِم أنْ آخُذ العِلاج؟

....

....

4- katab lii ad-ductuur waSfat muDaad Hayawii.

4- كَتَب لي الدكتور وَصْفَة مُضاد حَيَويّ.

....

....

5- 'ashAur be'alam fii ra'sii wa Aynii.

5- أشْعُر بِألَم في رَأسِي وعَيْني.

....

....

Exercise 3: Complete the conjugation of the verbs below in the present tense

English	Transliteration	Arabic	Pro
I start	'abda'	أبْدَأ	أنا
We start			نَحْن
You start (male)			أنْتَ
You start (female)			أنْتِ
You start (plural)			أنتم
He starts	yabda'	يَبْدَأ	هُوَ
She starts			هِيَ
They start			هُمْ

English	Transliteration	Arabic	Pro
I feel	'ashAur	أَشْعُر	أنا
We feel			نَحْن
You feel (male)			أَنْتَ
You feel (female)			أَنْتِ
You feel (plural)			أنتم
He feels	yashAur	يَشْعُر	هُوَ
She feels			هِيَ
They feel			هُمْ

Exercise 4: Match each singular in (**B**) with its plural in (**A**) to learn new plurals:

<table>
<tr><th colspan="2">B</th><th colspan="2">A</th></tr>
<tr><td>qurS</td><td>قُرْص</td><td>'awlaad</td><td>أَوْلاد</td></tr>
<tr><td>'alam</td><td>أَلَمْ</td><td>'aAmaal</td><td>أَعْمال</td></tr>
<tr><td>walad</td><td>وَلَدْ</td><td>'abnaa'</td><td>أَبْناء</td></tr>
<tr><td>Aamal</td><td>عَمَلْ</td><td>'aalaam</td><td>آلام</td></tr>
<tr><td>shughl</td><td>شُغْل</td><td>'aqraaS</td><td>أَقْراص</td></tr>
<tr><td>ebn</td><td>إِبْن</td><td>'ashghaal</td><td>أَشْغال</td></tr>
<tr><td>qalam</td><td>قَلَم</td><td>'alwaan</td><td>أَلْوان</td></tr>
<tr><td>lawn</td><td>لَوْن</td><td>'aqlaam</td><td>أَقْلام</td></tr>
</table>

Exercise 5: What does it mean?

English	Transliteration	Arabic
....	*wajh*	وَجْه
....	*'anf*	أنْف
....	*uThun (uThunaan)*	أذن (أذُنان)
....	*fam*	فَم
....	*Thaqn*	ذَقْن
....	*shaAr*	شَعْر
....	*raqaba*	رَقَبَة
....	*sen ('asnaan)*	سين (أسْنان)
....	*katef ('aktaaf)*	كَتِف (أكْتاف)
....	*TheraaA(TheraaAaan)*	ذِرَاع (ذِراعان)
....	*yad (yadaan)*	يَد (يدان)
....	*'eSbaA ('aSaabeA)*	إَصْبِع (أصابِع)

Exercise 6: Using the words below, fill in the puzzle with the meanings. Remember to go from right to left or up to down.

Down

2- for a period

Across

1- during

3- time (for counting)

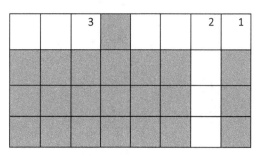

Exercise 7: Fill in the blanks using the vocabulary you have learned to make a dialogue

Adam: I have a bad sore throat.	A:......................... ....!	آدم: ....!
Dr. Khaled: When did it start?	D:..........................?	د. خالِد: ....؟
Adam: Three days ago.	A:.........................	آدم: ....
Dr. Khaled: Do you have any other symptoms?	D:.......................... ....?	د. خالِد: ....؟
Adam: I have a slight fever.	A:...........................	آدم: ....

Exercise 8: Fill in the blanks with appropriate words

1- men al-laazem 'an ———— le-doctuur.

1. مِن اللازِم أن ———— لِدكتور.

2- 'ayna ———— al'snaan men faDlek?

2- أين ———— الأسنان مِن فَضْلِك؟

3- kam —— men al-laazem 'an 'akhuth alAelaaj?

3- كَمْ —— مِنْ اللازِم أنْ آخُذ العلاج؟

4- katab lii —— waSfat muDaad Hayawii.

4- كَتَب لي —— وَصْفَة مُضاد حَيَويّ.

5- 'ashAur ———— fii ra'sii wa Aynii.

5- أشْعُر ———— في رَأسي وعَيْني.

Exercise 9: Give the plural of the words as in the first example

English	Transliteration	Arabic
head (heads)	raa's (ru'auus)	رَأس (رُءوس)
eye (eyes)	Ain (............)	عَيْن (............)
nose (noses)	'anf (............)	أَنْف (............)
cheek (cheeks)	khad (............)	خَد (............)
chin (chins)	Thaqn (............)	ذَقْن (............)
heart (hearts)	qalb (............)	قَلْب (............)
belly (bellies)	baTn (............)	بَطْن (............)
chest (chests / breasts)	Sadr (............)	صَدْر (............)
Another pattern		
tooth (teeth)	sen ('asnaan)	سِين (أَسْنَـان)
shoulder (shoulders)	katef (............)	كَتِف (............)
hand (hands)	yad (............)	يَد (............)
finger (fingers)	'eSbaA (............)	أَصْبِع (............)
foot (feet)	qadam (............)	قَدَم (............)
elbow (elbows)	kuuA (............)	كوع (............)

Exercise 10: Match each word in (**A**) with the appropriate meaning in (**B**)

B		A	
light		*mar-raat*	مَرّات
cure		*'aAraaD*	أعْراض
pill / tablet		*shadiid/a*	شَديد / ة
getting better		*Tafiif/a*	طَفيف / ـة
time (for counting)		*le-mud-da*	لِمُدّة
times		*khafiif / a*	خَفيف/ ـة
symptoms		*Aelaaj*	عِلاج
strong		*qurS*	قُرص
slight		*taHas-sun*	تَحَسّن
for a period		*mar-ra*	مَرّة
during		*khelaal*	خِلال

Vocabulary

I feel, أَشْعُر
'ashAur
antibiotic, مُضادّ حَيَويّ
muDaadd Hayawii
light, خَفيف / ة
khafiif / a
heavy, ثَقيل / ة
Thaqiil/a
fever, حُمّى
Hum-maa
cure, عِلاج
Aelaaj
medicine, دَواء
dawaa'
pill / tablet, قُرص
qurS
getting better, تَحَسُّن
taHas-sun
to get better, تَحَسَّن
taHas-san
Time (for counting), مَرّة
mar-ra
times, مَرّات
mar-raat
symptoms, أَعراض
'aAraaD
strong, شَديد / ة
shadiid/a
slight, طَفيف / ة
Tafiif/a
for a period, لِمُدّة
le-mud-da
It's necessary to, مِن اللازِم أن
men al-laazem 'an
during, خِلال
khelaal
prescription, وَصفة
waSfa
other / another, أُخرَى
ukhraa
pain, أَلَم

tooth (Teeth), سِن (أَسْنان)
sen ('asnaan)
shoulder (Shoulders), كَتِف (أَكْتاف)
katef ('aktaaf)
arm (Arms), ذِراع (ذِراعان)
TheraaA(TheraaAaan)
hand (Hands), يَد (يَدان)
yad (yadaan)
finger (Fingers), أَصْبِع (أصابِع)
'eSbaA ('aSaabeA)
chest, صَدْر
Sadr
elbow, كوع
kuuA
heart, قَلْب
qalb
belly, بَطْن
baTn
stomach, مَعِدة
maAeda
leg (Legs), رِجْل (أَرْجُل)
rejl (arjul)
knee (Knees), رُكْبة (رُكْبَتَيْن)
rukba (rukbatain)
foot (Feet), قَدَم (أَقْدام)
qadam (aqdaam)
back, ظَهْر
THahr
I start, أَبْدَأ
'abda'
fam
cheek (Cheeks), خَد (خُدود)
khad (khuduud)
chin, ذَقْن
Thaqn
hair, شَعْر
shaAr
neck, رَقَبة
raqaba

'alam

head, رَأْس

raa's

face, وَجْه

wajh

eye (Eyes), (عَيْن (عَيْنان

Ain (Ainaan)

nose, أنف

'anf

ear (Ears), (أُذُن (أُذُنان

uThun (uThunaan)

mouth, فَم

UNIT FIFTEEN

At the Bank

UNIT FIFTEEN

At the Bank

Contents

- At the Bank

- Vocabulary

- Culture notes

- Grammar usage

- Exercises

At the Bank

fii l-maSraf

في المَصْرَف

English	Transliteration	Arabic
Sami: Welcome. I'm Sami, from customer service. How can I help you?	S: marhaban, 'anaa samii, men khedmat alAumalaa'. 'ay musaaAda?	**سَامي:** مَرْحَباً؛ أنا سَامِي؛ مِنْ خِدْمة العُمَلاء؛ أي مُساعَدة؟
Adam: Hi. My name is Adam Jacob. I want to open an account at your bank.	A: 'ahlan, esmii 'adam yaquub. uriid 'an aftaH Hesaab Aendakum.	**آدَم:** أهْلاً؛ اِسْمِي آدَم يَعْقُوب؛ أريد أنْ أفْتح حِسَاب عِنْدَكم.
Sami: Saving account or current account?	S: Hesaab tawfiir 'am Hesaab jaarii?	**سَامي:** حِسابْ تَوْفير أمْ حِساب جَاري؟
Adam: Saving account.	A: Hesaab tawfiir	**آدَم:** حِساب تَوفير
Sami: How much would you like to deposit today?	S: kam tuHeb 'an tuudeA alyawm fii el-Hesaab?	**سَامي:** كَمْ تُحِبّ أنْ تُودِع اليَوم في الحِسَاب؟
Adam: I have 900 USD in cash.	A: maAii 900 dollar amriikyy naqdan.	**آدَم:** مَعي 900 دولار أمْريكي نَقْداً.
Sami: I'll get you an application form to fill out.	S: sawfa uHDer laka estmaraa; le-tamlaa' al-bayaanaat	**سَامي:** سَوْفَ أحْضِر لَك اِسْتِمارة؛ لِتَمْلأ البَيَانات.
Adam: These are my details.	A: haThehe bayaanaatii, tafaD-Dal.	**آدَم:** هَذِه بَياناتي؛ تَفَضّل.
Sami: You'll receive your ATM card within one week. You can use it for withdrawals, deposits, and payment of bills.	S: sawfa tastalem beTaaqat aS-Sarf el-aalii khelaal usbuuA, yumkenak behaa as-saHb wal-'eiidaaA,wadafA al-fwaatiir.	**سَامي:** سَوْف تَسْتَلِم بِطَاقة الصَّرف الآلي خِلال أسْبوع؛ يُمْكنك بها السَّحْب، والإيداع، وَدَفع الفَوَاتير

Adam: Is there a service fee for that?	A: hal hunaak maSrufaat lehaThehe el-khedma?	آدَم: هَلْ هُناك مَصروفَات لِهَذِه الخِدْمَة؟
Sami: No. only 3 USD a month for the On-Line banking service.	S: laa, faqaT 3 dolaraat fii ash-shahr lekhdmat al-bank el-alelktroni Aalaa al'entarnet.	سامي: لا؛ فَقَط 3 دولارات في الشَّهْر لِخِدْمَة البَنْك الألِكْتروني عَلَى الإنْتَرْنِت
Adam: Thanks a lot Mr. Sami.	A: shukran jaziilan ustaaTh samii	آدَم: شُكْراً جَزيلاً أسْتاذ سامي.
Sami: You're quite welcome Mr. Adam.	S: shar-raft ya ustaaTh 'adam.	سامي: شَرَّفْت يا أسْتاذ آدَم.

Vocabulary

English	Transliteration	Arabic
Customer service.	khedmat alAumalaa'	خِدْمَة العُمَلاء
'ayn khedmat alAumalaa' men faDlek?		أين خدمة العملاء من فضلك؟
bank	maSraf	مَصرَف
an account	Hesaab	حِساب
saving account	Hesaab tawfiir	حِساب تَوْفير
current account	Hesaab jaarii	حِساب جاري
Aendii Hesaab tawfiir fil-maSraf al-Aaraby		عندي حساب توفير في المصرف العربي
details.	bayaanaat	بَيانات
an application	estemaara	إسْتِمارَة
uriid estemaarat bayaanaat men faDlek		أريد استمارة بيانات من فضلك
he receives	yastalem	يَسْتَلِم
estalamtu kashf Hesaab men al-maSraf al-yawm		استلمت كشف حساب من المصرف اليوم

279

withdrawals	*saHb*	سحْب
deposits	*eiidaaA*	إيداع
machine	*maakiina*	ماكينة
hal hunaak maakiinat saHb wa eiidaaA qariib men hunaa?		هل هناك ماكينة سحب وإيداع قريب من هنا؟
transfer / s	*at-taHwiil / aat*	تَحْويل / تحويلات
paying	*dafA*	دَفْع
bill/ bills	*fatuura / fawaatiir*	فاتورة / فَواتير
daa'eman 'aAmal taHwiilaatii wa 'adfaA al-fawaatiir Aala al-internet		دائما أعمل تحويلاتي وأدفع الفواتير على الإنترنت
cash	*naqdan*	نَقْداً
card	*beTaaqa*	بِطاقة
hal yumken 'an 'adfaA bel-beTaaqa?		هل يمكن أن أدفع بالبطاقة؟
he opens	*yaftaH*	يَفْتَح
'aftaH baab say-yaaratii bel-remuut		أفتح باب سيارتي بالريموت
fees/ expenses	*maSruufaat*	مَصْروفات
Aendii maSruufaat kathiira fil-AuTla		عندي مصروفات كثيرة في العطلة
cashier / teller	*Sar-raaf*	صَرّاف
Sadiiqii Sar-raaf fil-maSraf al-Araby		صديقي صرّاف في المصرف العربي
ATM	*Sar-raaf 'aalyy*	صَرّاف آلي

Other Useful Vocabulary

English	Transliteration	Arabic
credit	e'temaan	اِئْتِمان
credit card	beTaaqat e'temaan	بِطاقَة اِئْتِمان
Aendii 3 beTaaqaat e'temaan		عندي 3 بطاقات ائتمان
check	shiik	شـيك
loan / loans	qarD / quruuD	قَرْض / قُروض
laa uHeb ash-shiikaat 'aw al-quruuD		لا أحب الشيكات أو القروض
accountant	muHaaseb	مُحاسب
director	mudiir	مْدير
lii Sadiiqa taAmal muHaaseba fii l-maSraf		لي صديقة تعمل محاسبة في المصرف
tax / taxes	Dariiba / Daraa'eb	ضَريبَة / ضرائِبْ
laysa hunaak Daraa'eb fis-sauudyya		ليس هناك ضرائب في السعودية
interest	faa'eda	فائِدَة
laysa hunaak qarD beduun faa'eda fii 'auruuba		ليس هناك قرض بدون فائدة في أوروبا
center	markaz	مركز
financial	maalii /a	مالي / ـة
maktabii fil-markaz al-maalii fil-madiina		مَكتبي في المركز المالي في المدينة
financing	tamwiil	تَمْويل
mortgage	rahn	رَهْن
uriid 'an 'aAref maAluumaat Aan tamwill 'aw rahn bayt men faDlek		أريد معلومات عن تمويل أو رهن بيت من فضلك
currency / ies	Aumla / Aumlaat	عُمْلَة / عملات
hunaak Aumlaat kathiira fil-belaad el-Aarabyya		هناك عملات كثيرة في البلاد العربية
wallet	maHfaTHa	مَحْفَظة
'ayn maHfaTHatii? kaanat Aala al-maktab!		أين محفظتي؟ كانت على المكتب!

Say it in Arabic

1- Where is the customer service desk please?

2- I want to open a saving account

3- Can I have an application please?

4- I usually have one deposit and many withdrawals in my bank statment a month

5- Can I pay by card?

6- Do I have to pay cash?

7- Is there an ATM machine nearby please?

8- I don't like loans or credit cards

9- I usually pay my bills online

10- I have a mortgage which I have to pay every month

Fill in the blanks with one of the new Vocabulary

1- *Aendii* .... *kathiira haTha ash-shahr besabab al-AuTla.*

2- *hal yumken 'an* .... *bel-beTaaqa?*

3- *uriid 'an 'aAmal* .... *men western union*

4- *laa* ....*baab ghurfatii Aendmaa 'anaam*

5- *Aendii* .... *tawfiir fii haTha l-maSraf*

1- عندي .... كثيرة هذا الشهر بسبب الإجازة.

2- هل يمكن أن .... بالبطاقة؟

3- أريد أن أعمل .... من ويسترن يونيون.

4- لا .... باب غرفتي عندما أنام.

5- عندي .... توفير في هذا المصرف.

<u>**Culture notes**</u>

Most of the Muslims around Arab countries and non Arab countries like to deal with banks who follow the (sharia law banking system), (sharia) is an Arabic word means (way or path). Shari'a deals with many topics which are addressed by secular law.

Grammar Usage

You have seen the employee when he said to Adam (*yumkenuka*) (يمكنك) which literally means (it is possible to you), as you see the verb is in the form of (he). As there is no pronoun for (it) in Arabic, that's why it's considered (he or she). Also you have learned how to use the same word but as (*men almumken 'an*) (من الممكن أن) which means (it's possible to), both of the phrases are used in spoken Arabic instead of (can you? / or you can).

Exercise 1: Complete conjugating the verbs below in the present tense

English	Transliteration	Arabic	Pro
I bring	*'auHDer*	أحْضِر	أنا
We bring			نَحْن
You bring (male)			أنْتَ
You bring (female)			أنْتِ
You bring (plural)			أنتم
He brings	*yuHDer*	يُحْضِر	هُوَ
She brings			هِيَ
They bring			هُمْ

English	Transliteration	Arabic	Pro
I receive	*'astalem*	أسْتَلِم	أنا
We receive			نَحْن
You receive (male)			أنْتَ
You receive (female)			أنْتِ
You receive (plural)			أنتم
He receives	*yastalem*	يَسْتَلِم	هُوَ
She receives			هِيَ
They receive			هُمْ

English	Transliteration	Arabic	Pro
I open	'aftaH	أَفْتَح	أنا
We open			نَحْن
You open (male)			أَنْتَ
You open (female)			أَنْتِ
You open (plural)			أنتم
He opens	yaftaH	يَفْتَح	هُوَ
She opens			هِيَ
They open			هُمْ

English	Transliteration	Arabic	Pro
I spend (money)	'aSref	أَصْرِف	أنا
We spend			نَحْن
You spend (male)			أَنْتَ
You spend (female)			أَنْتِ
You spend (plural)			أنتم
He spends	yaSref	يَصْرِف	هُوَ
She spends			هِيَ
They spend			هُمْ

English	Transliteration	Arabic	Pro
I pay (money)	'adfaA	أَدْفَع	أنا
We pay			نَحْن
You pay (male)			أَنْتَ
You pay (female)			أَنْتِ
You pay (plural)			أنتم
He pays	yadfaA	يَدْفَع	هُوَ
She pays			هِيَ
They pay			هُمْ

English	Transliteration	Arabic	Pro
I withdraw	'as-Hab	أسْحَب	أنا
We withdraw			نَحْن
You withdraw (male)			أنْتَ
You withdraw (female)			أنْتِ
You withdraw (plural)			أنتم
He withdraws	yas-Hab	يَسْحَب	هُوَ
She withdraws			هِيَ
They withdraw			هُمْ

Exercise 2: Translate into Arabic

1- I'd like to open a bank account please.

…………………………………………………………………………………

2- Do you have a credit card?

…………………………………………………………………………………

3- Do you have any interest on the saving account?

…………………………………………………………………………………

4- Do you have any interest on the current account?

…………………………………………………………………………………

5- I want to open an account without any interest please.

…………………………………………………………………………………

6- Do you have car loans?

…………………………………………………………………………………

7- When can I receive my credit card please?

…………………………………………………………………………………

8- I want to take a car loan.

………………………………………………………………………………

9- When can I receive my ATM card please?

………………………………………………………………………………

285

Exercise 3: What does it mean?

English	Transliteration	Arabic
....	khedmat alAumalaa'	خِدْمَة العُمَلَاء
....	Hesaab tawfiir	حِسَاب تَوْفير
....	Hesaab jaarii	حِسَاب جاري
....	bayaanaat	بَيانات
....	estemaara	اِسْتِمارَة
....	as-saHb	السّحْب
....	al-'eiidaaA	الإيداع
....	at-taHwiil	التّحْويل
....	dafA	دَفْع
....	naqdan	نَقْداً
....	maSruufaat	مَصْروفات
....	Sar-raaf	صَرّاف
....	Sar-raaf 'aalyy	صَرّاف آلي

Exercise 4: Fill in the blanks with appropriate words

1- uriid 'an ———— Hesaab Aendakum.

١. أريد أنْ ـــــــــ حِسَاب عِنْدَكم.

2- ———— tawfiir 'am ———— jaarii?

٢- حِسَاب تَوْفير أمْ حِسَاب جَاري؟

3- kam —— men al-laazem 'an 'awdeA?

٣- كَمْ ـــ مِنْ اللازم أنْ أودع؟

4- hal hunaak —— lehaThehe el-khedma?

٤- هَلْ هُناك ـــــــــ لِهَذِه الخِدْمَة؟

5- laa, faqaT 3 dolaraat fii ————

٥- لا؛ فَقَط 3 دولارات في ـــــــــ.

Exercise 5: Choose the correct Arabic meanings for the English words below

A- Loan

3- مَوْعِد mawAed	2- سَبَبْ sabab	1- قَرْض qarD

B- Finance

3- مَوْعِد mawAed	2- سَبَبْ sabab	1- مال maal

C- Financing

3- تَمْويل tamwiil	2- مال maal	1- مَوْعِد mawAed

D- Credit

3- فائِدَة faa'eda	2- حَسَنًا Hasanan	1- إِئتِمان e'temaan

E- Wallet

3- للأسَف lel'asaf	2- مَحْفَظة maHfaTHa	1- رَهْن rahn

F- Currency

3- عُمْلَة Aumla	2- مَحْفَظة maHfaTHa	1- رَهْن rahn

G- Transfer

3- فائِدَة faa'eda	2- تَحْويل taHwiil	1- إِئتِمان e'temaan

Exercise 6: Match each word in (A) with the appropriate meaning in (B)

<table>
<tr><td colspan="2" align="center">B</td><td colspan="2" align="center">A</td></tr>
<tr><td>credit</td><td></td><td>qarD</td><td>قَرْض</td></tr>
<tr><td>credit card</td><td></td><td>Sar-raaf</td><td>صَرّاف</td></tr>
<tr><td>check</td><td></td><td>muHaaseb</td><td>مُحاسب</td></tr>
<tr><td>loan / loans</td><td></td><td>e'temaan</td><td>إئْتِمان</td></tr>
<tr><td>teller</td><td></td><td>betaaqat</td><td>بِطاقَة</td></tr>
<tr><td>accountant</td><td></td><td>shiik</td><td>شيك</td></tr>
<tr><td>director</td><td></td><td>maalii</td><td>مالي</td></tr>
<tr><td>interest</td><td></td><td>tamwiil</td><td>تَمْويل</td></tr>
<tr><td>finance</td><td></td><td>rahn</td><td>رَهْن</td></tr>
<tr><td>financial</td><td></td><td>mudiir</td><td>مُدير</td></tr>
<tr><td>financing</td><td></td><td>faa'eda</td><td>فائِدَة</td></tr>
<tr><td>mortgage</td><td></td><td>maal</td><td>مال</td></tr>
<tr><td>currency</td><td></td><td>Aumla</td><td>عُمْلَة</td></tr>
<tr><td>wallet</td><td></td><td>maHfaTHa</td><td>مَحْفَظة</td></tr>
</table>

]

Exercise 7: Fill in the blanks using the vocabulary you have learned to make a dialogue

Adam: Hi. My name is Adam. I want to open an account at your bank.

A: ....

آدَم: ....

....

....

Sami: Saving account or current account?

S: ....

سَامي: ....

..........................? ؟.........................

Adam: Saving account.

A: ....

آدَم: ....

Sami: How much would you like to deposit today?

S: ....

سامي: ....

..........................? ؟.........................

Exercise 8: Write an email in Arabic to your bank asking them to change your address "Address = عُنوان". Use this verb: to change = يُغَيّر

....

....

....

....

....

....

Exercise 9: Can you find the 4 Arabic meanings for the words in the word square below?

1- transfer

2- bank

3- cashier / teller

4- accountant

5- account

ي	ت	ح	و	ي	ل	ر
أ	م	ص	ر	ف	م	ج
ك	ص	رّ	ا	ف	أً	ا
م	ح	ا	س	ب	ر	ف
ق	ح	س	ا	ب	ن	و

Exercise 10: Using the words below, fill in the puzzle with the meanings. Remember to go from right to left or up to down.

Down

2- loan

Across

1- cash

3- mortgage

VOCABULARY

Customer service., خِدْمَة العُمَلاء
khedmat alAumalaa'

an account, حِساب
Hesaab

saving account, حِساب تَوْفِير
Hesaab tawfiir

current account, حِساب جاري
Hesaab jaarii

details, بَيانات
bayaanaat

He receives, يَسْتَلِم
yastalem

an application, اِسْتِمارَة
estemaara

withdrawals, سحب
saHb

deposits, اِيداع
'eiidaaA

transfer, تَحويل
taHwiil

paying, دَفْع
dafA

bill/ bills, فاتورة / فَواتير
fatuura / fawaatiir

cash, نَقْداً
naqdan

He opens, يَفْتَح
yaftaH

fees/ expenses, مَصْروفات
maSruufaat

cashier / teller, صَرّاف
Sar-raaf

ATM, صَرّاف آلي
Sar-raaf 'aalyy

expenses, مصروفات
maSruufaat

credit card, بِطاقَة اِئْتِمان
betaaqat e'temaan

director, مُدير
mudiir

tax / taxes, ضَريبَة / ضرائِب
Dariiba / Daraa'eb

interest, فائِدَة
faa'eda

financial, مالي / ـة
maalii /a

financing, تَمْويل
tamwiil

mortgage, رَهْن
rahn

currency, عُمْلَة
Aumla

wallet, مَحْفَظَة
maHfaTHa

I bring, أُحْضِر
'auHDer

I receive, أَسْتَلِم
'astalem

I spend (money), أصْرِف
'aSref

I withdraw, أسْحَب
'as-Hab

bank, مَصْرَف
maSraf

crrency, عُمْلَة
omla

loan, قَرْض
qarD

accountant, مُحاسب
muHaaseb

Get your copy of

Part 2

Arabic Script

The Easiest Arabic Reading & Writing

Course

ABOUT THE AUTHOR

The author graduated from Al-Azhar University, which is considered the oldest continuously functioning university in the world. This mosque and school complex was built during the reign of Fatimid Dynasty, with the doors opening in 972 CE. In the 1960s, Al-Azhar University expanded its curriculum to include modern subjects such as applied sciences, engineering and a college of medicine as well as linguistics and Islamic studies.

For more than a thousand years, students have traveled from around the world to study at this prestigious university. In recent decades, many American scholars have studied the Qur'an and Hadith at Al-Azhar. Al-Azhar has not only served as a center of Arab philosophical, religious and scientific learning, it has also served in producing many patriotic leaders for the whole Arab nation. For these reasons, graduates of this university are well known for their good knowledge.

The author has the pen name of Dr. Adam Yacoub. He is an experienced Arabic linguist in addition to his career for several years in teaching Arabic as a foreign language, editor, and proofreader.

CPSIA information can be obtained
at www.ICGtesting.com
Printed in the USA
LVHW102343140319
610751LV00003B/41/P